Best Spiritual Literature

Best
Spiritual
Literature

Vol. 9
2024

Edited by Luke Hankins, Nathan Poole, & Karen Tucker

ORISON
BOOKS

Best Spiritual Literature (Vol. 9, 2024)
Copyright © 2024 by Orison Books, Inc.
For information regarding the copyright for the individual works that appear in this volume, please consult the Acknowledgments & Permissions pages (pp. 144–145).

ISSN: 2833-1168
ISBN: 978-1-949039-52-8

Orison Books
PO Box 8385
Asheville, NC 28814
www.orisonbooks.com

Best Spiritual Literature is digitally archived by EBSCO*host*.

Cover photo by olpo. Used courtesy of Shutterstock.
Cover design by Luke Hankins and Addison Skigen.

Manufactured in the U.S.A.

ORISON
BOOKS

CONTENTS

FICTION

NONFICTION

ABOUT *BEST SPIRITUAL LITERATURE*

Best Spiritual Literature (from 2016–2021, titled *The Orison Anthology* [ISSN 2380-7776]) collects the finest spiritually engaged writing that appeared in periodicals in the preceding year. The series is released in print and is digitally archived by EBSCO*host*.

In addition to reprinted material, the anthology also includes new, previously unpublished works of fiction, nonfiction, and poetry by the winners of The *Best Spiritual Literature* Awards.

Editors of periodicals may submit work for consideration each year from August 1 – November 1. The *Best Spiritual Literature* Awards are open for submissions each year from May 1 – August 1. Consult www.orisonbooks.com/submissions for the latest guidelines.

Sarah Ghazal Ali

ISM

The name of God is sufficient
for me. Merciful, beneficent—I want
to want little else. I shouldn't
say that I'm there yet, wanting little
else but the name, not when
nothing flusters me like an image,
Mount Tamalpais in acrylic salmon
and sage, the hue, the brown eddies
of my own eyes, every staggering sight—
but I hush them, my zealous eyes. I recite.
Said the angel *recite in the name*
of your lord. I come from
a people who begin with the name,
who absent the face, who efface
and know it faith. Who say bismillah
before breathing, before leaving. The name
is in the name, *ism*, in the name,
in Arabic. You see, I don't see
to believe, don't desire a babbling bush
or shrinking sea-halves. I am trying
not to worship my eager eyes.
Doesn't the mantis shrimp see more
color than any other creature alive?
A poet says our long gone loves remain
lateral, unseen but quiet beside us, perhaps.
I admire that belief in a love that doesn't leave.
Here-ism, or remainism, more convincing
an -ism that beckons than inflicts
a rift. I believe in the weakness of my species,
the lure of our many malevolent -isms.
I won't name them. For love of the name,
I learn instead all that I can of what grows

softly, without seeking praise.
O linden, lichen, mulberry underripe,
fragrant fisted peony. O flower medicinal,
emollient aloe, I call you by your name,
bismillah, O divine unseen whose name
I know, ism of isms, remain here,
invisible and I will call to you, crouched,
recognizing each green
by touch by name by sense unseen.

Originally published in Guernica

Sarah Ghazal Ali

Pantoum with Ecclesiastes

There is no god
save him. All will be effaced
save his face. In my mind's
private eye: sockets bright with black.

For him, I efface
each image I've hungered for. Condemned
to the public eye, I reach into my own sockets.
The eye never has enough of seeing.

Each image I've eaten
meaningless, meaningless.
Have you seen enough of me?
There is nothing new, not me, not you.

Meaningless, meaningless.
All will be effaced. Oh, save me
from the loneliness of believing
there is no god.

Originally published in The Sewanee Review

Winner of The 2023 *Best Spiritual Literature* Award For Fiction

Sionnain Buckley

Like a Prayer

Father Tony held a Bible like a baby bird, spoke to us mostly like baby birds too, barely above a whisper as if we might blow away with his breath. I got it in my head, in those days, that Jesus sounded like that too—the kind of gentle firmness that quiets a crowded room so they won't miss a word. The ten of us, two months away from our confirmations, had felt our religion classes starting to take on a new weight. Instead of relying on the calendar, the passage of ordinary time, Father Tony was pointing the lessons at us. We sat in a circle on the rug of a borrowed second grade classroom, sweaty from a full day of middle school boyhood, and it didn't matter how softly he spoke to us—the last thing we wanted was to be looked at closely.

"Let me just give you this passage here," Father Tony said, his fingers grazing his pages. The others couldn't sit still, kept adjusting, fidgeting, tapping their thumbs on their pant legs. But I believed him—that he was giving me something—and I couldn't look away. I was fourteen and had never seen a man smile at a book, or laugh with earnest pleasure. He rubbed his jaw with the heel of his hand and some strange corner of me flared like a warning. "Luke, Chapter 2—the boy Jesus in the temple," he said, and an urge rose like a sudden belch, to reach out and feel the spot on his face that he had just touched.

"How about you, Luke?" he said, and it took me a beat to realize he was looking at me. "Your namesake—do you want to read this one?"

He held his Bible out, the book suspended in the middle of our circle, and I couldn't very well not take it. His fingers brushed mine as I took it from him, and I thought of the pages, how many times he must have turned them, tender and breakable as skin.

"While we read, let's think about these adults—his parents, the teachers—and their reactions to Jesus. Do you think they take him seriously? He asks questions, but he has answers too. Do they trust him? Are they afraid of him?" Father Tony nodded at me to begin.

"And the child grew…" I started, my voice catching and then finding itself again. One of the other boys snorted in the back of his throat, the requisite acknowledgment of a voice crack. The others were quiet, looking at their feet and pretending to listen, but across the circle Father Tony was listening. Each time I paused and looked up he was watching, nodding to indicate that I should continue, and so I read, barely hearing myself, only processing his eyes on my face and a blurry image of Jesus, younger than me, being listened to in the temple by older men, learned men, just so.

After school let out the next Tuesday, I found my usual waiting spot at the empty bike rack, away from the idling buses and the packs of kids inhaling exhaust fumes. The biggest boys terrorized the sixth graders, sidling up behind groups of girls half their height and shouting in their ears to watch them jump. The security guards glared at them from the steps until they dispersed, laughing, to hide behind the trees.

Once the bus kids and the walkers went off in their various directions, the ten of us gravitated towards each other and started the walk to St. Andrew's, the Catholic school a few blocks away where Father Tony would be waiting for us. None of us were friends, so we walked in a nebulous blob arranged by status, one of the shouters leading the pack, and me trailing in the back with the quiet kids. Still out of sight of the church, the boys in the front competed to see who could shock the others, spewing increasingly longer trains of swears and slurs.

"God hates fags!" Danny, the shouter, said merrily.

Brian, who wore lacrosse shorts and tube socks that left only his bony knees exposed, looked thoughtful for a moment. "Jesus fucked Mary."

"His mom?" Craig said, from just in front of me.

"No, the prostitute, duh," Danny replied.

"I doubt it. Dude was definitely a virgin."

"Father Tony is a virgin."

"You think priests really aren't going over to the nuns for that shit?" Brian said.

"Not Tony, dude."

As soon as we turned the corner onto Elm Street and the spire of the cathedral rose between the trees, the group abandoned their debate, falling silent except for Danny at the front, who began to rap under his breath quietly.

At fourteen, in our public middle school, it wasn't cool to believe in God. That the Yankees would win the World Series, that Mrs. Baumfeld was the worst teacher in the school, that Juuling was cool and feeling up girls was cooler: these were things to believe in. It didn't matter that half the kids we knew were Catholic, a quarter were Jewish, and the rest were something rather than nothing—it was easier, at fourteen, to be a heathen.

But I couldn't turn it on and off the way the others did, an hour on Sunday mornings, an hour on Tuesday afternoons, blasphemy all the rest. Standing between my mom and my older brother during mass, the familiar prayers spilling out of me like sweat, without effort or will, it felt out of my hands whether I believed or not. Father Tony stood at the pulpit, looking small and too far away, but his voice rang through the speakers and up through my feet, closer than ever.

When we made it to the doors of the Catholic school, the boys at the front clambered inside and took off running, racing to the second-grade hallway. The rest of us tramped behind, their shouts echoing back at us through the empty halls, the lights dimmed like we were trespassing.

"Hello, hello!" Father Tony greeted us when we made it to the classroom, the other boys looking flushed and windswept and pleased with themselves on either side of him. He motioned us over to the rug, shaking each of our hands as he always did at the beginning of each class. We stood for the prayer, hand in hand as Father Tony insisted, then wiped our sticky palms on our t-shirts as we collapsed onto the rug.

"Today we're going to go over your chosen confirmation names. Who wants to start us off?"

We went around the circle, reading from our handwritten patron saint worksheets, explaining our choices with the bulleted lists we'd pulled from Wikipedia the night before. Four out of the ten of us had chosen Saint James, another three had picked Saint John.

When it came to my turn, I hesitated over my notes. "Saint Anthony," I said, my neck flushing.

"An exceptional choice," Father Tony said, his eyes catching mine. "If I do say so myself."

"My mom says I'm always losing things." I attempted a shrug. Each of my bullet points justified the choice, but as I read them I couldn't look up at him, too worried that it was readable on my face, that Anthony of Padua was good and fine but was not the Anthony I was naming myself for. It was Father Tony who had taught me about faith, his voice I heard when I read my assigned Bible chapters, his face I pictured when I thought of Christ himself.

"I pray that he will allow nothing to be lost on you," Father Tony said solemnly. He turned to the kid next to me, nodding as he stumbled through a story about Saint Blaise, and I watched the line of his jaw, the muscles of his neck disappearing under the high collar of his shirt. Under the black fabric, hidden from us, were thin shoulders, the suggestion of collarbones, and what else? My own body, shifting under me every time I blinked, was bad enough. I thought of Brian and Craig on the walk from school, arguing over whether Jesus had been a virgin, whether Father Tony was too. It was a series of thoughts I wasn't sure I could follow, not here across from him in broad daylight, surrounded by the rest of them, only a single sheet of paper filled with his name in my lap.

It took me the entire length of the car ride home to ask the question that was lodged in my throat. When my mom pulled into the driveway and turned the car off, I kept my seatbelt on, stalling. "So…" I said, forcing myself to begin. "I have a weird thing to ask."

"Mhm?" She flipped down the visor and looked at herself in the mirror, baring her teeth in a flash of white before hiding them again, then turned to face me.

"Do you think Jesus ever like, dated anyone?"

She chuckled, the kind of soft laugh I'd been hearing all my life. "Well, I don't know about dating being a thing back then."

"But like, you know. Do you think he was ever in love or whatever?"

She looked over at me, and I looked away quickly, staring intently through the windshield at the blank gray face of the garage door, streaked with dirt.

"Well, he was a person, which makes me think there's no real way around it."

"Not everyone falls in love," I whispered.

"No, sure…" she said, tilting her head in my periphery. "But if most people do, then he probably did. Some say Mary Magdalene was his wife. I'm just saying I wouldn't be surprised."

Neither of us said anything for a few long moments, and then my mom clicked her seatbelt off. "I hate to be that mom, but is there a reason you're asking? Like—a love reason?"

Finally I looked over at her, summoning my best horrified look. "Are you asking me if I'm in love, mom? Really? Am I allowed to just be interested in history? Or theology? Or whatever?" I turned my back to her and stared out the side window at the empty yard and the empty street.

"Oh, honey. I'm just momming you." she said, touching her fingers to my shoulder quickly. "Father Tony's probably a better bet for those kinds of questions anyway, you know."

"Yeah, you're probably right." I pulled out my phone and told her I'd be in in a minute, and she left me in the quiet capsule of the car, my ears ringing from the slam of the door.

She was the one who had never been in love. That's what she always told my brother Tim and me whenever we asked why she never married, why she decided to adopt two kids at thirty-three without waiting any longer. There had been a story or two about guys she had dated in college or just after, but they weren't very exciting, and it always made me feel strange to think of her before we existed, oblivious, just a little older than Tim, kissing someone not unlike him maybe, and laughing her same laugh.

Maybe that had been Father Tony too. I could see the two of them—in another life, before whatever now was—driving out of town and parking the car in some secluded spot, catching each other's eyes in the dark, leaning their shoulders against each other for warmth, then the rest of themselves too, maybe, all the while spinning out thoughts about what it could mean if this feeling in their stomachs, this one right now, was love.

Something moved in the corner of my eye, and I looked to see my mom leaning out the front door, turning her palm up to the sky as if to say *what's up* or possibly check for rain. I nodded and waved her away, and when she disappeared inside, I flipped my phone back into my pocket and closed my eyes. The car's silence pressed in around me, and I imagined the darkness behind my eyelids was that other car's darkness, tried to imagine the warmth of it, the quiet that comes right before the inhale, and someone beside me waiting for me to turn and look.

When the ten of us arrived at the double doors of the St. Andrew's school building the following Tuesday, Craig's mom was waiting for us with a grocery bag full of pretzels and mini bottles of Gatorade. We thanked her for the snacks as Craig avoided eye contact, then we walked politely down the hallway together with her trailing behind. Each week, on a rotation, one of our moms came to help with class, although there wasn't much for them to do. Most of the time they sat near the window, reading articles on their phones, or if it was Rodney's mom, knitting the same long blue hunk of blanket she'd been working on all year. Craig's mom was the only one who brought snacks, so naturally she was our favorite.

It was a rule—the mom-chaperones—a preventative measure that was part of the catechism trainings, and Father Tony didn't complain. There were too many stories, a new one every week if you looked for it, although none of us did. It had never happened in our parish anyway. Still, we let the knowledge sit with us in the room, in the shape of our mothers, or just beside us, like an eleventh kid, invisible but exactly our size.

After our opening prayer, Father Tony led us into our discussion for the day: the history and the purpose of the sacraments, now that we were preparing again for one of our own.

"After the sacraments of initiation come the sacraments of service, which are Holy Orders—like yours truly—and Matrimony. And we have an expert in the room for that one as well," he said, and behind him, at the window, Craig's mom laughed. "What do you say, Lisa? Give us an insider's view of marriage." He twisted around on the rug to look at her.

He sometimes resembled a child, sitting cross-legged next to us with the primary-colored rug pinned under his knees. He looked like that then—gazing up at Craig's mother, waiting for her words. The others around me glanced over as well, betraying their curiosity. Only Craig continued to stare into his lap, picking at his cuticles and frowning.

"Well… let's see," his mom began. "I'd say it's challenging, and it's no wonder it's a sacrament of service." She chuckled at herself. "What I really think is that it's easy to convince ourselves that we know our spouse better than anyone. And that's true in some ways." She paused, looking over at Craig, then back at Father Tony. "But a successful marriage—being in a good marriage—it's an admission that we don't know everything, and a promise to keep learning."

Father Tony raised his eyebrows, his ears lifting slightly with the movement. We were the only two still looking at her. Around me, the others were digging at crumbs lodged in the rug, or watching Father Tony for what came next, but he sat paused there, turned at the waist, his eyes drifting closed as if meditating on Craig's mother's words.

He had explained to us once, years before, when we were still too young to grasp metaphor, that priests don't marry because they are married to the church instead. It stuck in me the way childhood images do, and ever since then, despite myself, I imagined him retreating to our church at night, dimming the lights and walking up the aisle to the sanctuary, lying down on the plush red carpet at the foot of the altar and sleeping inside his spouse. I knew this was a silly thought, knew, in fact, that he had a room in the rectory next to the church building, with the two other priests who worked at St. Andrew's. There was a kitchen where they cooked dinners together, and a living room with a donated TV and a pool table, normal things. But still, I couldn't help but picture him up at the altar of the empty church, curled on the ground in his collar and black slacks, his shiny shoes placed neatly at the base of the steps.

Finally, after a long minute of silence, Father Tony opened his eyes and turned back to face the circle, his eyes landing on me, moving over my face like he was seeing me anew. He smiled, and took a breath to speak, and God if I could have turned away I would have, but there he was in me like a barb, too many layers deep to count, and no hope of going back.

I still think of that church sometimes, and how I would go to him there if I could—pulling open the heavy door in the dark, stepping softly on the tile and kneeling in front of his sleeping form. The bottoms of his feet would face the pews, resting on each other like small animals, pale and clean, and I'd have to suppress the urge to reach out and hold them. I wouldn't want to wake him, but he would sense me there eventually, blink his eyes open, and sit up on the top step, clasping his hands between spread thighs. I would be fourteen again in front of him, no helping it at all, shrinking until I became something he recognized, until he smiled at me like that again.

"What do you need?" he would ask, in that soft voice, with sleep still stuck in his eyes. I couldn't tell him, couldn't speak at all, not here on my knees looking up at him, but he would know anyway. He would rest his palm on my forehead, his fingers reaching up into my hair. My eyes would close instinctively at the pressure of his hand, the weight of his blessing pushing me down, bowing me down, onto the cold tile and below it, where the earth lay damp and packed close and waiting.

James Roderick Burns

Duns Scotus

> *...this air I gather and I release*
> *He lived on; these weeds and waters, these walls are what*
> *He haunted who of all men most sways my spirits to peace*
> **–Gerard Manley Hopkins**, "Duns Scotus's Oxford"

It was a very curious moment—as odd, in its way, as the time he sketched himself upside down in the unmoving surface of a lake (feet and hat-brim crisp and angular, but eyes lost in a mass of shadow) or when he swam so long at Parson's Pleasure he could hardly tell where the river ended and his heavy limbs began.

On the cusp of the moment he felt himself moving forwards, outwards, as though detached from time and the singular concerns of the day. From young man to older, middle age to youth, even young man to boy again. All met each other's passing looks with calm and curiosity, and no little sense of wonder; their regard flowed in between like a delicate, semi-opaque liquid. Looking back, he would not fault himself for such a fancy. It was at this moment, after all, that his own torn halves were sewn back together: priest and poet, low sensual creature and being of light; long parted, grating continually like the ends of an unset bone, now indivisible as a harlequin's chequerboard, angles and colours perfectly seamed and stitched into harmony.

No, he must hold it simple and clean in his mind, for there alone it made sense. That place and no other.

*

When he could not sleep, and pain churned through his roiling stomach, despite a surfeit of dull food, his mind would expand beyond the dormitory fug, the manicured seminary lawns and fine-built school with its squadrons of fledgling Catholic foot-soldiers, and reach for the wild embrace of the fells. Ribblesdale, Pendle Hill, the sweet confluence of three rivers; moor. pool and waterfall. As his body cramped, his soul moved out through the landscape unfettered. The next day he would be felled by exhaustion, but his mind—the part of him least damaged by the depredations of the world—would compensate, digging through layers of ingrained text for the correct response. The effort left him fragile, desperate for the rough buffeting of the moor upon his senses.

"'Opkins!"

Coming back—a classmate? Father Duffy, that brusque voice a treacherous guide to the quicksilver mind behind it. Gerard groped for an answer. As ever, he was an excellent student, a scholar if not an aesthete at heart. His fellow seminarians could rely on him for the quick escape, though some were leery of the star of Balliol. He looked askance at his classmates now and then, most from old Catholic families with Latin bred in their bones. Others looked down on him, for at several inches above five feet he looked up to almost everyone. They were good men, but not generally worthy of being looked at. He kept his silence, living for the last few hours of light on the fells. The swirl of leaves on a peat-brown pool bobbed just out of reach.

Let him think on his walks, then, as day wound to its close. He would answer, and not think of the college, or of his friend. Only calm leaves on a pool.

*

As a student, Gerard had not given much thought to chapel, beyond his normal weekday attendance and joining the other young men with gowns and worn psalters. He had moved from prep school to college as easily as a man who had lived on a street for his whole life, but never entered a particular building. On being invited in, he found it slightly odd—perhaps an unexpected kink in a hallway, light falling strangely on the staircase—but on the whole reassuringly familiar. They said the chapel's layers of pink and yellow sandstone resembled streaky bacon, and he was minded to object to such an earthy image; already he leant towards incense and vestments, a whole world of ritual beyond the promise of the arched doorway, and his heart moved silently beyond such a cavil.

There were only a few steps, and those well-worn and shallow, so it was a surprise to all when D stumbled up them like a swan flailing in a storm, and fell on one shoulder against the brick. His collar-bone gave way with a crack, and Gerard rushed up.

"Are you alright?"

He placed a hand near the shoulder and the other boy winced, cried out.

"Tell the Master I'm taking him to his room," he said, though to whom he had no idea. Under the other arm he gave a gentle, upwards pressure, and they lurched back across the quad to their stair. Up the rail, his clammy palm trailing behind, through the oak and quickly onto the blankets. He propped D's head with a pillow, removed his shoes.

"You rest while I fetch matron." When they returned, she ushered Gerard across the hall, and closed the door.

Baths were achievable, it seemed later that day, though he imagined a great circus-like performance levering even the slight body in and out of heavy porcelain, but shaving was impossible.

"I can lather alright, old man," D said, moving his good hand in languid circles as though it held the badger-hair brush, and he was trying to manoeuvre thick curds onto his cheek, "but a stroke or two and I'm a bloody mess." He turned his face to the window. Gerard saw one or two red, angry slits rounding the jaw. His friend lowered his eyes. "Would you mind awfully?"

"Now?"

"Yes. Why not?"

"I—well,—"

From outside came the noises of evening—footsteps on gravel, voices lingering round the stonework. The ancient door creaked then banged in the college gate. Tomorrow was lectures, a tutorial. How could he be so selfish?

"Of course."

Gerard patted his friend on the shoulder.

*

"Just—yes, angle your head down a bit. Turn away."

He had finagled a pot of boiling water from the buttery, much to the keeper's amusement, and run with it back up three flights to their floor; whipped up the soap-cake to a pile of standing froth, before dampening his friend's whiskers and handing him a loaded brush; laughed along with his evident discomfiture, dabbing away foam-spots that landed beyond the towel's collar; and stood now, razor in hand, its curving blade hot under his fingers where he had rinsed it.

"Gerard, come *along!*" D giggled and shook off a few more droplets. He waggled his good hand backwards, towards his friend's shadow.

For a moment more Gerard lingered, the steel angled between his fingers, then made his first stroke. The razor's edge bit into the first patch of whisker and D flinched, stiffening. It gave a sharp rasp, cutting cleanly. He wiped the blade on a towel, dipped it once again in the steaming pot, then paused.

He wished above all not to hurt him, to simply be of service. An earlier slash, pinkish at the crest, showed through the layer of soap like a parted lip, and with the next stroke Gerard cut gently around it. It was odd, this movement of the shaving-hand away from his body; awkward, like tracking collar studs in the looking glass, or pushing charcoal across a sketchbook with eyes on a line of trees. D shrank at the touch, and Gerard apologised, but his friend brushed him off.

"Ready for my handsome side?"

With his good hand he fingered the plane of his now-shaved cheek, the bump of chin (only half smooth), then laughed again.

"I shall never get to lectures at this rate!"

But he rose obediently and sat down on the stool, offered up his face. Gerard fluffed up his chin and cheek, where the old foam had run to water. Outside the voices had passed and all was quiet. No sounds of carriages on the cobbles; not even a bird settling, the porter's first sortie around the gravel.

With a trembling hand he reached out. There was no sudden moment of awareness, no second of flight beyond the window as a bird slowed for the roof. No branch knocked against his conscience, or distant voice startled him awake. He watched as the slow curve of the blade dipped towards the standing foam, and in the second of hesitant air, his friend's face break out in half a smile.

Oh, how his heart leapt!

Still the blade moved towards its odd combination of slide and crunch, touching yet not quite touching flesh. D paused, head cocked, the smile lighting the unshadowed half of his face with all the grace of the angels. It was a sweet countenance, full of life, but its sweetness was not what moved Gerard's heart. It was happy, too, despite the burden of injury—open, and trusting, and free of every snideness and the world's grim patina of experience. But yet its openness was not what captivated him.

As his slow hand reached the target and the blade bit, he knew fully what drew him to this face. The knowledge pierced the rim of his soul, puncturing its resistance, and a warm flood of hunger poured in.

Somehow he got through the rest: stroke, towel and laugh, the thanks of his friend, their rough putting-away of stool and water-pot, the washing out of the brush. He even managed a calm goodnight, and wished him restful sleep before the work of the morrow began with the birds.

But when he talked of these things with Newman—in the most glancing, roundabout way—and was received into the Church, he knew what must come of such terrible beauty and every one of its traces.

One evening, soon after, he hefted the papier-mâché box, took out the letters with their heavy freight of words, and fed them one by one to the flames. He would write no poems for seven years.

*

There was no obligation for him to dwell on such things. He knew that barring snatched moments of companionship, and charged loneliness on moor or fell, his life in the long progression to priesthood would brim over with duty: pastoral, theological, pedagogical, liturgical; duties plain and duties overwrought with meaning, duties sacramental in intensity, wrapped round his mind and heart like tender snarls of wire. He did not need to think so, and yet he must.

From the silent quad's moment of truth to another, this loud as a torrent breaking through the orderly landscape of his mind: the burn. In his closed eye he saw the extended holiday after years of study, the wise release of novices by their masters to a world without pressure, shorn of duty for a few short weeks, both time and men released into the wild.

They departed for Scotland on a steamer, collars tucked away, changes of clothes and books (always books) packed in satchels, then watched as England departed like a shucked fruit-rind, the peel falling away in one unbroken, satisfying curl. As the land receded a sea mist came up, and his companions departed for the warmth of the cabin, but Gerard remained on deck, fingers tingling with the damp and cold, to watch the line of the prow pushing back waves that slapped musically against the hull. It was not his usual escape, and in an odd way pulled him out of time. He remained in it, conscious of the holiday and its purpose, but no longer of it—moving as he did between past and future, with his present a nest of complex thoughts winding round and about in a complex shape. Or perhaps he was of it, but no longer in it. The boat chugged into a white and featureless future, bright as thought, and perhaps as fleeting.

Suddenly he laughed and knocked his small fist on the rail. Such ruminations, and on the first day of the holiday!

He went inside with the rest of them.

*

After Greenock, and another steamer, they arrived at their fortnight's row of houses overlooking the Firth and began to plot the adventure. He did not mind such organisation; someone—perhaps a man whose head was less likely to be in the clouds—should make the most of their stay, and that required a firm hand. There would be trips to Arran (a miniature Scotland, someone said), to Edinburgh and Glasgow, though these held little interest. He did not wish to bump and chuff his way across the country to peer at sandstone through a blanket of smoke. What held him fast was an outing to the Loch.

"Do you fancy it, Hopkins?"

He did, and averred to Kerr and his brother that it seemed a most charming prospect.

"Better than the cities, I should say," his friend agreed. As they moved from stage to stage through the clerical life, the young men (gradually growing thicker skins, and perhaps becoming wiser) met old friends passing through new destinations. The Kerrs would accompany him at different stages, and he was glad of their company, particularly Henry.

"Loch Lomond it is."

In his room he set up his half-dozen volumes between two bookends carved in the shape of King Charles spaniels, their bulging wooden eyes beginning to split and crack, and smiled. In his mind the lake had all the untapped potential of a distant unexplored fell, a new and unexpected pool shining through parted ferns.

In a couple of hours they were tramping through heather to the shore of the loch. Henry Kerr was familiar with the terrain, his family having holidayed there, and he and his brother had a yen to walk to a small island they remembered from their childhood.

"Y'ull be alright on your own, then, Gerard? We shall meet up after lunch, back along—"

Kerr gestured at the steep slope, winding through gorse-land, to the station.

"Of course. We'll get tea."

They nodded and shrugged on their backpacks, struck away round the shore without a backwards glance. He remained still for a moment and mopped his brow in the sun, then set off in the opposite direction. If the guidebook was to be trusted it was only a few miles round the other way; a highlight of nature, a sight to set right the senses, or so the writer's rather windy prose claimed. In truth, his senses were already aflame; he revelled in the solitary landscape.

It took longer than advertised (or perhaps his legs were simply shorter than the journalist's) but eventually he rounded the last inlet and stopped, dropping his backpack to the ground. The canvas rasped on stony soil, and from inside came an ominous clunk, his glass water bottle thumping against earth. He did not notice. His legs followed the pack down onto a pack of bent ferns. He ran fingers through his hair, dabbed his brow then stopped moving. It was a sight he knew would never leave him.

Those things at which you look hard, he knew, look hard back at you—from whorls of ice creeping across a milk-churn, left out overnight for the farmer to stack on his cart, to waste water flashing up the sides of a drain, its rough quartz sides suddenly piercing as the sunrise. He knew, looking back, there could be no erasure. Though the words lay silent—quite hidden, for the moment, he was sure—they waited like a deepening pool behind a natural dam, poised for the time when they could burst through and out into the world, released in great leaping runnels like the burn itself, as it turned and tumbled down the mountain.

Here was another moment of wonder; stilled in time, yet ever-living. He was looking at a miracle from the wrong end up; standing, as though struck blind at the sight—though he never felt further from lost vision—at the foot of a mountain of water slicing apart a mountain-range of rock.

The burn was quick, mobile and multi-hued, its sides bright and foam-capped where they churned against stone and grass, its depths dark and roiling with moving shadows slow as cream poured into black tea. Both solid and liquid, the waters slammed through heath and moor to a churning pool at their foot. Their noises rang out in tandem—wet roll and flat splash against the rocks; slow gurgle and reedy sizzle, as all the force of water ran square into the calm of the lake.

Gerard stood, lost to himself, as the minutes slipped into hours. Eventually he considered a drink, but somehow his hand would not lift the canvas flap. He considered his hat, as the sun was surprisingly hot, but a little warmth seemed unimportant beside such ever-rolling spectacle.

The Kerrs found him some hours later, pink and sweating. They hauled him to his feet.

"Fine scene, eh Gerard?" one said. He was not sure which.

"Indeed—indeed. And—ah, your—little island?"

"Splendid, yes. Have a sip of this, old man."

They put their arms around him, one side and the other, offering a leather-lined bottle. The water inside was cool, but as they stumped back along the bank, an awkward six-legged beast, he knew the flood in his memory was cooler, and bided its time in the wildness and wet.

*

When he was not tramping fells, sketching in his notebook or attending to duties he regarded as wholly necessary (but not perhaps best suited to his temperament) he could be found in the library. At Stonyhurst, as at Balliol, it became a second home; with sun struggling to penetrate leaded windows, autumn winds buffeting the latches, or hail pocking against glass, even the coming and going of the sconces' mean light did not matter. Under his hands the volumes grew, their touch and smell almost as dear as the waft of moorland pools.

With his duties complete, the afternoon's walk shot down by looming grey that soon erupted into showers, Gerard made his way to the library to see if a promised treat had come. The Badeley collection, gifted by a church lawyer some years before, had taken its time being categorised and readied for use, the bindings repaired and sheets preserved, as though legions of rough characters would soon be pawing through its pages!

The librarian had assured him it would soon be available, and may have some utility. He mounted the stairs and shook the rain out of his hair, ran a finger round his collar. He was sure to steam for a while in his bay by the window, but what of it? His fingers were always gentle in the pastures of print.

The librarian had outdone himself: a note, and cloth-wrapped, the largest volume of the bequest, Duns Scotus's *Scriptum Oxoniense super Sententiis*. He sat, reverently unwrapping it, readying himself for study. There were inklings, he knew, in his wider reading of the medieval theologian: theories of incarnation and the senses, each thing unique unto itself, and the glorious, wide surrounding world a blessing from God—not the curse his teachers seemed to maintain, some mountain-range of traps and boulders, unseen crevasses waiting to swallow the unseeing traveller—so that his fingers shook as he turned the pages, his eyes pressed close to ink warmed with anticipation.

Head bent and lost in theology, he remained as the storm outside whipped up tapping branches and dumped a month of rain onto the tiles.

The librarian pottered, rearranging notes in a catalogue, tidying his papers then sitting for a while with his feet on the rungs of his desk, simply listening to the wind and water. The young man was intense. Soft and small, with no physical presence at all; at the librarian's school he would have been trampled underfoot by the lowliest member of the team. But he gave off a glow of bright intelligence, goodness too, he thought; from the small shoulders, set in earnest, the lowered head, he gathered an impression of grace.

After a further hour it was time for the building to close. The librarian walked over.

"Scotus, eh?"

Hopkins looked up. His eyes were tired, but still bright interest sparkled there.

"Yes—thank you so much for preparing him. Most enlightening."

"You can continue tomorrow. I'll put the volume up."

"Thank you."

He rose and gathered pen and papers, recapped the bottle of ink. Its cork squeaked in a momentary lull of wind.

"What do you take as Scotus's main theme?" asked the librarian.

Gerard jumped, then covered his nerves by tugging at his jacket. He had not anticipated questions.

"Well, I—I suppose earlier thinking, or other thinking, perhaps, that the world is a distraction and an evil path away from divinity is mistaken. The world—all that rain! the fells, pools and waterfalls, even those branches knocking on the glass—is a symbol of God, a way of approaching the divine through the senses of man. That's what I think, anyway."

"And the Society?"

"The Society?"

"What do your masters make of the famous Franciscan?"

"Oh! I am not sure."

They reached the short flight of stairs leading outside. The librarian held the door for the young man to pass.

"I believe they regard him as an eccentric—hardly central to our thinking, but harmless all the same. You should be fine with further study of the bequest, should you wish."

Gerard looked at him from halfway down the stairs. He was an older brother, with a calm, lined face, full of simple wisdom and authority. The departing light cast happy shadows about its crags. Without worries he smiled, thanked the librarian again and turned to make his way into the storm. Though the wind was dying down, freshets of water and the odd blown twig flew here and there before his face. He caught one on a blast of air as the library door snicked home.

*

In the end, he realised, it was not one moment but many—indivisible in import, in lasting purpose, but separable with just a small tweak of his mind, like beads on a wire pulled apart to reveal the silver thread connecting them, snapping back on release.

But what to make of it?

He supposed, for all the marvellous fancies of his work—the thought, taut and compact, drilling for meaning through dense layers of sound and rhythm; the grand, reaching passages; lives wrestled from obscurity, from the dark loss of the grave to God's light—there was only one image that lasted, flowing in and out of them all: water. He did not need its clear, sacramental force (though he felt God move through it), its symbols, its song; the substance itself picked him up, a stick dropping into the current, and washed him to glory.

Gerard stopped. The path of his vocation, long and gnarled as a tree-root burrowing through soil, beautiful in its own way; his crisis of art, poems stopped-up and burnt, yet pressed over years into a kind of living mulch, till at last he could hold them back no more; the torrent of verse spilling through myriad letters to friends, ending who knew where. These things comforted him. In thinking of them, he understood.

He returned again to the image of his youth.

Rounded hat, clean feet, the suggestion of high branches sketched in the background. Even his nose, he saw, was sharp, the line of a contemplative lip clean as his pencil could make it. But his eyes—these lay hooded in shadow. Why had he drilled the lead down so, obscuring his soul? Why hatched out those windows? Only the tiny currents of the surface could tell.

He folded the drawing back along its accustomed lines, slipped it into the bequest's next volume. There was so much to do—so many volumes, leaves as yet uncut—and beyond such work lay the crooked world still, scarred with the wicked lines of the flood, to reconcile to the one who loosed the waters.

Originally published in Vita Poetica Journal

Mark Christhilf

Overtures on Some Unanswered Questions

I

There is something in me, I am not sure what, but I know it dwells in me. Suns and moons pass through it—rains, snows, whole seasons. The living depart, the young are born, and yet it remains unchanged. I do not know what it is, but it sees me seeing. It hears my voice speaking, hears even what I am now telling you, and watches my living as from a great height. In it I am dust in the radiance of dust, one spark lit from the grand burning. In it my fears and desires are yours. All faces form one face. And everything that happened once goes on happening. Civilizations rise, decline, and fall, and in each one the departed are struggling to answer the same question of what it is and of how we have it.

All I know is I want more of it, more and more and more, no matter what the day or hour, no matter where I am or what I am doing, I need it as an addict needs a fix. It is as if it were life itself, and without it I am lost, locked out of myself, bereft and abandoned, and because it comes and goes like the wind, I have chased it with coffee, tea, or wine, with waiting and listening, austerities, with solitude and loneliness. Night after night, vigil after vigil, the search makes me what I am. And this I am sure of: it goes with me to the end. After that, who knows?

II

The last night of summer. Faint is the odor of earth. Dry to the touch is the grass. Deep in the inward darkness a voice is counting as if there is not much time. To live is to be gathered out of the earth which one shares with the living, and it would be enough except for the voice measuring all one has done against what remains to do. What is it but the mind's response to the possibilities which consciousness confers. Companions on our temporal journey, they are invisible to everyone but ourselves—yet they perpetually demand existence. To make them real is to write our story, and through the power of will, they enter time. Always dissatisfied with who we are in the present, they ask for a return on our talents, abilities, and capacities. When we fail to realize them, once passed over, they linger on with the mournful face of regret.

The possibilities are the truth in us, looking for a being in whom others find kinship and confirmation of their hope that the good exists. Isn't that why truth gets in the way of an honest person? And why, no matter how much sweat we have given to any project or relationship, truth will not fully accept its success, disdains all smugness and conceit, and scorns complacency. Breaking through the walls of the house, it reminds us of the times we lost patience, indulged laziness, and willful desires, and knowingly betrayed our purpose. Before the potential inherent in truth, everyone is an imposter, and due to the need to think well of ourselves, many avoid or deny it and bear enmity toward those who pursue it. It seems that's why truth follows our undertakings with these questions. *Could you have done even more? Are you giving one hundred percent?* Because its possibilities are unlimited, to fulfill one only leaves another, thus there is always more to do, and more that might have been done. Our truth, then, exists not as certainty, but as a moving target, always ahead, drawing us on toward the unknown future, and coming to seem an unpayable debt, it leaves us always unfinished. It seems our destiny is to be reborn again and again.

III

It has streets of its own, lined with trees and houses that belong to it alone. Fields and forests found nowhere else, broad lakes, and ocean beaches. Its many faces, bright as violets, are all desperate for our attention, wanting us to live among them again, to share once more their joy, sorrow, or conversation. What is it but memory, casting its spell, playing the past over and over, demanding our moments, our hours, our breath, and in its realm all that once happened continues to happen. Yet everyday it grows more crowded and becomes a populous city, for from briefest encounters spring the phantoms that go with us until we die. To live is to relive. But why?

Are the memories who we are? Do you cherish them, striving to keep them fresh and vital, take photos to help, save souvenirs, keepsakes from your travels, or evidence from past accomplishments? Do you behave as if your past is real—or only an illusion? There's little doubt that memories are grist for the mind's mill, help reason make sense of experience, and provide the landmarks by which we make our way through the ever-changing organization of the world. But they have a strange power to crowd out the present, so that the work before us becomes difficult, and they come willy-nilly, without reflection, often in a flood, a reverie, which interrupts the direction of thought.

Memory seems to insist we are our past, and our identity more fact than possibility. Much of their power lies in the fact that our future is unknowable, uncertain, and its projects may never happen, whereas the past seems reliable and safe, imparts weight and solidity, and assures us it is who we are. But what happens to those who cling to their past? Don't they often become complacent, accepting themselves just as they are, without feeling any need for improvement? Overemphasis on memory may lead us to take the ashes for the fire: to be increasingly focused on our private lives and less able to participate in the living whole. It may embed us solely in the dimension of spacetime so we forget the judgement of eternity which informs life with meaning.

It seems the purpose of memories is our transformation, to show us not who we are but who we could be. By bearing witness to the fears and desires to which we once succumbed, they expose our weaknesses, shortcomings, and flaws, for not only do they bring pleasure but also remind of wrong decisions, selfish behavior, transgressions against others; and because they reenact repeatedly such mistakes, they indicate the way to correct them, signaling the work that must be done to make ourselves better and more magnanimous. Ideally, memory points to the way ahead, revealing how much room there is within us for another, larger life. It can be a liberator as well as an enslaver. The decision is up to us.

IV

It's no one thing, it's the way it all fits: the ocean breathing in its shoreline, the rivers swelling in springtime to drain the rain-filled fields. It's the communion of the water with the sky as it faithfully accepts the changing colors. It's the harmonious wedding of natural things that makes me want to call it love. But the skeptic in me forbids that, seeing nothing but matter in motion; and claims that everything we see and are is only atoms falling through space, combining and recombining.

Do you too form an argument between yes and no? Do you see too much for denial, but too little to be sure? And when you decide on one position, does doubt begin to buttress the other, nixing your attempt to establish any sort of firm conviction? Can it be that affirmation produces negation, and negation, affirmation? That the two trade places naturally in our mind, just as summer and winter slowly yield to one another? Do you strive for a balance between your positives and negatives, for one harmonious outlook? When you feel love is the meaning, are you being superstitious? Old-fashioned? Romantic? Do you consider faith a gift? A mystery? Can it emerge from acquisition of knowledge? And when you feel gratitude for the simple goodness of things, who do you thank in the midst of your unknowing?

V

In the depth of winter when snow grips the land and icy winds bite the flesh, I often notice bare trees following the river which winds through a nearby meadow. To think of their roots drinking beneath the white cover, and to see their naked limbs reaching skyward, can bring to my mind this silent prayer: *O let me live to see these trees green again.* Whereupon a voice from somewhere asks: *To whom are you speaking?* And sheepishly I reply: *To no one. No one holds that power over me—either I live or not.* And find myself then a contemporary, facing a total darkness, bereft of the myths that make God omnipotent and disposed to intervene in the prayer's life. Yet despite what reason tells, pray I did. But why? From what motive?

Does prayer form naturally in the subconscious from thirst for life and fear of death? Is it from a sense of helplessness before life's power to change our fate abruptly and completely—through accident, financial loss, or crippling illness? Is it from the need to lose ourselves in some greater whole, which then becomes for many a personal benefactor who grants good fortune, and even helps us to overcome harmful instincts? Such prayer can lead easily to idolatry and a false sense of security: we give up power over ourselves and the freedom to control our own fate. For what is God but a possibility who depends on us for existence. Isn't s/he the one who needs our help, who waits imprisoned in matter, waits in the cells and neurons of the mind, powerless to emerge unless through our efforts? Isn't God asking to be born in us—to have us for companions?

Yet if you are like me, you may find it hard to make return on the God within, because the mind is a wild thing, full of tricks and illusions, and prone to pursue its own inclinations. That may be where prayer has a part to play, by helping us to concentrate, to marshal the energies of the mind and apply them to the task at hand. And prayer can yield an increase in consciousness which clarifies life's complexities. Not only that, but without it we all too quickly forget the good done for us by others, or easily overlook the work they are doing to give purpose to their life and make a contribution. Prayers of thankfulness can keep us from taking things for granted, and from viewing the earth as but a useful resource. So, if nothing else, to pray on occasion serves as a mnemonic—like tying a string around your finger to remember what's important.

Originally published in The Potomac Review

Kwame Dawes

Cathedral

When my soul was hurted deep within,
And I'm warring to be free desperately
 –**Bob Marley**, "Give Thanks and Praises"

After "Cathedral" from Subterranea *by Sally Gall*

For years I have mapped the crowded forest
of my emotions, which is not even the word—
it is the quagmire of fears, of the texture
of my days. The note scribbled on a piece
of cheap tissue; rough with slivers
of unprocessed pulp—simply reads:
"You believe you are interesting—it is
a lie." There is a truth that startles us—
the truth we uncover in the dark grotto
of a cathedral—the only word to name
the high walls, and the looming avenues.
Imagine a commissioned artist, building
contraptions and scaffolding to lift
the aching bones of the last great duty,
the art that will outlast generations;
imagine this as the first view of the task
ahead—an artist mapping the contours
of the uneven walls, composing a stomach,
a nipple, an eye socket, a blade of grass,
a pool of stagnant water, against the markings
of nature; the boulevards of stone, the rockface,
the way light falls to the ground, the perfect
moment calculated by priests and seers,
to fall on the deep scar in the earth.
Think of a healed wound, an open mouth,

Kwame Dawes

a bowl for aromatic leaves and petals,
twigs and precious stones; the perfect
revelatory moment while praying
in this shadow hall, carved out by centuries
of flood waters. It occurs to me that there is no great
beauty in my expressed holiness, my glowing
face after the mountain top, that every whisper
of adoration is a cesspool of insecurity;
that people will carry a secret unto death,
that a good night's sleep—empty
of dreams, is as clear a truth as there ever
will be. To face this understanding
is to know that nothing is assured.
I shout out, a gut-wrenching howl—the echo
continues for as long as I will listen.

Originally published in The Adroit Journal

Moira Egan

Velar

She said that faith is her anchor
but I heard anger.

Fragile, fraught faith,
bells and beeswax candles a base-

less base, frankincense
and myrrh, common sense

thrown
out the stained-glass window.

Those characters
we studied in the Minster

windows, transluced
as through a membrane, luteous.

A medieval monk with spectacles
round like vintage Elton's.

Who knew that kind of vision was possible
back then? Her son a suicide, impassable

the life, ever unable
to translate love from the cradle

to where he was. Once
I touched a page of vellum

made of fetal calfskin. Buttery, as they say
in the trade.

Moira Egan

Disruptive to the systems, anger
or anchor.

Both velar. One voiced,
one voiceless.

Originally published in The Hopkins Review

Jeff Hardin

A Reverence

I call them my people, but they
belonged to hollows and hilltops,
to orchards and pews, to sandbars
and the dank entrances of caves.
They knew where quail bedded down
and to rub three leaves together
to stop a bee's sting. Some things
we now abide they called blasphemy,
but mostly they steered clear and let
others decide for themselves. Quiet
of a morning stilled the mind, cleansed
the soul. And they talked like that—
cleansed the soul—for they believed
one day they would stand account.
They belonged to time, too, and felt
a buoyancy in it, poised like a bobber
plunked down near a tree's fallen
crown where the water, dark green,
was scripture read with a steady eye
toward a moment lengthening into more
of itself until something seized from
underneath, and then death and life,
taut-lined, went wide-running and fierce.

Originally published in The Ilanot Review

Shadab Zeest Hashmi

Rumi and the Clock of Shams Tabrizi

A tree in the vicinity of Rumi's tomb has me transfixed. It isn't the tree, it is the force of attraction between tree-branch and sunray that seems to lift the tree off the ground and swirl it in sunshine, casting filigreed shadows on the concrete tiles across the courtyard. The tree's heavenward reach is so magnificent that not only does it seem to clasp the sun, but it spreads a tranquil yet powerful energy far beyond itself. It is easy to forget that the tree is small. I consider this my first meeting with Shams.

Of average human-height, the tree is non-descript, other than how its heavenward reaching creates an embrace that enriches and enlarges everything around it, so that motion ripples out of stillness, light edges shadows. In a moment such as this, the senses deepen spirit; words fail, words fail. All that we know evaporates, we are left with spirit. Here is the limit of knowledge, the Sufis teach us; no amount of book learning alone can bring us closer to the Divine than the spirit engaged in making a wide embrace. The Divine is an experience, and knowledge is only a part of it. If there is one word that comes close to describing this, it is love. But of course, the word is insufficient. No single word in conventional language can contain love. Poetry, arguably, owes its existence to the impossibility of defining love in the dictionary. In Maulana Rumi's case, it was Shams who brought this awakening, this great desire for the Divine beloved that colored every thought, action and word that was to come out of him in the future.

The disruption that Shams caused in Rumi's life became a legend. Shams appeared as if out of nowhere, challenged the limits of Rumi's mind and the untapped potential of his soul. The only way to true spiritual maturity, he taught Rumi, is through the heart: a heart that is "broken open."

Within a matter of days, some say 40, Rumi was transformed from the persona of an established scholar, a well-respected teacher, to an ecstatic poet, one to whom a door was suddenly opened and who was blinded and overjoyed by the light that came through. This, for Shams, was not enough; their spiritual synergy, a great blessing as it was, was insufficient yet for Rumi to reach the next level; separation was a necessity. According to William C. Chittick, in *Me and Rumi: The Autobiography of Shams-i-Tabrizi*, derived from written conversations between Shams and Rumi: "On more than one occasion he (Shams) implies that it would be best for him to leave, because Rumi was not yet mature enough to take full benefit from him. He says, for example, that he went to Aleppo because Rumi needed to be cooked by separation (3.220). When he did return, the fruit of separation was clear, because Rumi took much benefit from him: "One day of his companionship is equal to a year of that (earlier) companionship" (3.223). Rumi may be alluding to the role of Shams in a famous line that is often attributed to him by scholars of Persian: "The fruit of my life is no more than three words—I was raw, I was cooked, I was burnt." Perhaps Shams left because Rumi was now cooked and needed to be burned. Suddenly it was not a coincidence that Rumi was now forty, the traditional age of spiritual maturity."

Love traverses the domains of the heart, mind, spirit and the body. To Sufis such as Shams, understanding the Qura'an and prophetic tradition in the truest sense, is to understand all the ways how this great tradition is a language of love, a highly complex, dynamic, multifaceted force with mercy at its core, "Ar-Rahaman" ("The Supremely Merciful One") being one of the foremost names for God. Shams himself had had no shortage of book learning, but he considered it only a basic step. Chittick says, "The stories and anecdotes told in the later literature often make Shams out to be a spiritual genius, contemptuous of book learning and ignorant of the Islamic sciences. The discourses show that there is little basis for this view. In fact, Shams knew the Quran by heart and used to make his living as a teacher. He had studied jurisprudence (fiqh)—the science of the Shariah, the religious law—and even in Konya he spent time in the company of jurists. He certainly looked with contempt on superficial learning and the pretensions of the Ulamah."

At first Shams destabilized Rumi by openly challenging his scholastic approach to faith, calling out his complacency as a theologian. Perhaps the greatest teaching Shams brought to Rumi was an appreciation of paradox—a philosophical and spiritual level one can arrive at after a deep reading of sacred literature and immersing in meditation. Paradox (especially as reflected in *Al Asma ul Husna* or *The Beautiful Names of God*), balanced with praise, is the hallmark of Sufi wisdom. Rumi blossomed as a mystic poet as he became more and more aware of paradox, sharing with Shams words and silences, attachment and separation. Paradox was to become one of the most dynamic elements of Rumi's poetry.

Why exactly Shams arrived in Konya, why he would repeatedly disappear and eventually how he disappeared for good, his body never to be found for certain, will remain a mystery. What is clear is that he played a major role in leading to enlightenment one of the most remarkable mystic poets the world has known.

Shams's grave in Konya, nominated to be a UNESCO world heritage site, is in a beautiful mosque. But of course, no one knows if he's really buried there. In Chittick's opinion, "A rather late report says that he was murdered by jealous disciples with the collusion of Rumi's son Ala'aDin, from whom Rumi seems to have been estranged (at least after the departure of Shams). Those who follow this theory locate his tomb in Konya, not far from the tomb of Rumi himself. Others claim that he died in 1273, and that for centuries his tomb was known in Khuy in Iran. There are also tombs attributed to him in other parts of the Islamic world, thus reinforcing his mythic stature. Lewis has argued convincingly that nowhere near enough evidence exists to suggest that Shams was in fact murdered."

The tree in Maulana Rumi's tomb/Museum complex strikes me as a dervish—arms raised to the heavens in ecstasy—mirroring the essence of Shams, showing how to integrate the mind, body, and spirit via the paradoxically "vulnerable-powerful" heart, the part of us that must be broken open for ultimate enlightenment. As I walk through the mosque structure where Shams is said to be resting, I feel a beautiful peace settle within. It is midday, a partly cloudy summer day. The mosque has an abundance of lovely wooden windows and chandeliers that look like bouquets of white tulips. The aesthetics are a subtle reflection of the cultural crossroads that this place once was—the seat of the Seljuk empire, and before that, Byzantium.

The thing that really captures my imagination, is a grandfather clock, in fact multiple western-style clocks with pendulums in the mosque, reminiscent perhaps of modern Ottoman sensibility. The rhythm of the pendulum's sound and motion is a continuum of sorts, subdued five times a day by the "Azaan" or call to prayer; this locking in and freeing time is strangely an apt metaphor for Shams and Rumi. The time that they found together in the pursuit of the sacred, the time that stirred envy and suspicion in many, created controversies and ultimately was a source of maturity for Rumi– was brief, only a few months in all, but ironically contributed to our understanding of eternity through Rumi's verse.

The wood carvings are not too ornate but embellished enough for the visitor to appreciate the light entering through the various sources. Shams means "sun" in Arabic. Readers of Rumi know how well he applied the sage's name as a metaphor for light. His full name was Shamsuddin Mohamad Tabrizi. "Din" means "chosen path" or "religion." Shamsuddin stands for "the light of the way."

Shams's main message is that Love is its own language, the finest one to understand and speak of God with—superior by far to the languages that the intellect can conjure, echoed by Rumi in his famous lines: "Trying to explain Love, the intellect fell down in the mud like an ass—Love and loverhood can only be explained by Love. The sun is the sun's proof; If you must have proof, then turn not your face away from it."

Originally published in 3 Quarks Daily

Winner of the 2023 *Best Spiritual Literature* Award For Nonfiction

Kristin Kovacic

Litany

1. In Honor of the Wound in the Left Knee

Circa 1970; left kneecap; approximately ¾ inches long and ⅛ inch wide; shape of an amoeba or the State of New Jersey; light in color, smooth in texture.

In the course of researching Catholic saints and the religious orders founded in their names, I come across the Litany of the Sacred Wounds by Saint Clare of Assisi, founder of the Poor Clares. The litany is a list of five prayers, each dedicated to one of the wounds Christ suffered in his crucifixion: Right Hand, Left Hand, Right Foot, Left Foot, and Side.

If you are a Catholic (and I am not, though I live in a repurposed Catholic church), you know the Sacred Wounds by heart. If you have seen an image of Jesus nailed to the cross, the wounds are self-explanatory, except perhaps for the side wound, inflicted by the lance of a Roman soldier piercing Christ's upper abdomen to test if He had truly died (and famously probed by Doubting Thomas after the resurrection to test if He truly lived).

Clare was the first woman to write the rule of her own order, meaning she composed its spiritual practice. In her litany, she draws the attention of the person in prayer to each of the wounds in turn, reading the body of Christ like the chapters of a book. Clare's litany invites veneration as well as supplication—to worship each wound and to make a special request in its name. *By this holy and adorable wound,* she writes, invoking

44

the impaled right palm, *I beseech you to pardon all of the sins that I have committed by thought, word, and deed.*

I am arrested by *adorable*, a word deconsecrated, like the church I live in, and fallen in connotation from *divine* to *darling*. Though it may be blasphemous and truly offend the devout, the prayer provokes me to contemplate the significant wounds on my own body, of which there happen to be five. I wonder if they could be adorable in the sense Clare means—worthy of my concentration and veneration—and not in the sense inflicted upon me as someone who has inhabited a woman's body for sixty years—*attractive*, or God help me, *cute*.

I am drawn, in other words, to thinking of the body as a text, as it surely was in the early Middle Ages when St. Clare was composing her litany. For a thirteenth-century visionary, the image of Christ's body was more legible than the Bible. And Clare, like other penitents, used her own body primarily to express her devotion, famously shearing off her hair as a renunciation of worldly preoccupations, then founding an order whose deprivations of the body were so extreme she had to fend off many attempts (by powerful male clerics) to modify them.

The body is, of course, the instrument with which one perceives the body—a book that reads itself. I could title it, meaning no disrespect, The Five Wounds of Kristin. I could begin at the beginning, Chapter One, the Left Knee, the first wound of conscious memory.

*

Every happy childhood has an alley—a street rarely used by cars but accommodating the vehicles and games of children. Like every other alley in Pittsburgh, ours was nameless and on a hill. Unmaintained by the city, the alley was in an ever-evolving state of degradation, its poured asphalt pocked with gouges emitting hard pellets of gravel. It took a good six inches of snow, packed down, to turn the alley into a run that didn't tear up your sled. Too steep for hopscotch or baseball, the alley was for careening your bike, trike, Big Wheel, skateboard, unicycle, pogo stick, roller skates, or scooter, down its treacherous slope. The alley featured an open sewer grate at the top—from which the intrepid would fish out fetid baseballs—and a weedy lot we called The Rat Place at the bottom. A rule of the order of our neighborhood mothers was *Don't ride down the alley!* which we ignored at our thrilling peril. Many bicycle spokes were lost to the alley, many tires, many teeth.

My own wound was more prosaic: on foot, a tumble down the cascade of gravel during an epic game of Release. The fall itself was unremarkable, but I remember, at six years old, my genuine shock at how easily my skin tore and how solid the alley was, the barrier between me and the hardest things in the world alarmingly thin. And then the blood, covering my knee and pouring down my leg, a river with no discernible source.

Until my mother, summoned by my open keening, lifted me up and placed me on the kitchen table, the first and last time I ever sat upon that sacred hygienic plane. With a dish towel, she deftly cleaned my knee, revealing a constellation of cinder-filled cuts surrounding a deep, pulsing gash. Doused with Bactine and pinched together with Band-Aids, the wound disappeared from view, then she set to staunching my sobbing with some gentle chiding. *No reason to cry.*

When I contemplate this wound, I recall the reservoir of calm that was my mother, by any measure the most placid in the neighborhood. I recognize that as a child I was as free to stray (I was not *riding* down the alley when I fell), as I was certain to be saved (even if I had been). From this wound I understand the foundational comfort I took from being released and tethered in just that way, the reassuring balance of my mother's distance and proximity. Many of my own choices as a mother—including some that likely retarded my career—were made in the mind's eye that's still on that linoleum table, watching my mother bent to her solemn task.

By this adorable wound, still visible through a light stocking and traced with curiosity by more than one lover, I beseech you, God I don't believe in, to restore my mother's serenity to her. At eighty, the anxiety she has banked for everyone's comfort has flooded forth, washing out all peace. She calls me to ask when I will arrive, which pill goes into the afternoon box, what it was we were talking about when she called five minutes ago. From my new loft in an old church, I reassure her: Friday, the pink one, nothing much, no reason to cry.

By virtue of the wound on my left knee, I ask forgiveness for forgetting, for periods as short as an hour I don't have and as long as a decade I scarcely remember, that the work of love is incorruptible; it cannot be replicated; it cannot be phoned in. I am doing it now, imperfectly, yet I request an intercession. Please tie my mother to the solid, sordid earth again and resurrect her to herself for the rest of her days. Amen.

2. In Honor of the Wound in the Left Forearm
July 1985; back of the left forearm, beneath the elbow; approximately 1 in. long and ¹⁄₁₆ in. wide. Shape of a barely arched eyebrow or the blade of a scythe; light in color; smooth in texture.

My mother's hand shook so violently when she wrote the check—for $1200, the largest in her lifetime—her bank branch called, suspecting fraud. She had just purchased my wedding dress, a scaled-down but still opulent rendition of Princess Diana's ivory silk taffeta confection, complete with swirling ballroom skirt and billowing, tulle-filled sleeves, cinched just above the elbow.

She had offered me the money in cash—for the dress, the reception, everything—if we would just elope. *Think of what it could buy*, she said reasonably, *a down payment on a house, a new car.* I was twenty-one and couldn't hear her. Or rather, what I heard was her unwillingness to play her role, Mother of the Bride, for which she was entirely unsuited. I didn't want her to be practical. I didn't want her to be shy. I wanted her to transform, as I would transform, in my wedding gown. Turning down her offer, I dragged my modest, frugal parents through the whole ordeal—the shower, the invitations, the flowers, the minister and chapel (though we weren't churchgoers), the church hall, the dinner, the cake, the cookie table, the D.J., the dancing, the open bar. But the part I truly cared about, to the point of extorting my mother to tremors, was The Dress.

Never again would I desire anything so extravagant. I needed, it seemed urgently imperative, to look not just like a bride, but like *the most beautiful woman on earth.* I felt that if I could pull off this image, as abstract in my mind as God, for one day, my beauty, which even then I suspected was a vanishing asset, would be forever preserved in memory—mine, my husband's particularly, and those of 126 admiring guests. This absurd ambition overtook me, and the moment I stepped into the gown at the bridal boutique and caught a glimpse of that inchoate ideal in the mirror, I (and my mother) were done for.

Within these delusions was the haunting suspicion that I had no business getting married at all. This was also patently true; I was twenty-one years old. But two conflicting certainties possessed me—that I was too young to marry, and that Jim was whom I would marry. My most coherent thought at the time was *might as well get it over with.*

But first I had to register as the most beautiful woman on earth, and The Dress was my ticket to the claim. After clearing things up with the bank, The Dress was irrevocably mine and sent for alterations (given the exorbitant price, we had to purchase the floor sample). Jim and I then set off to bicycle across Europe for the summer, a pre-wedding trip that tested our forthcoming union in the fiery furnace of foreign travel, tent camping, and extreme sport.

The wound was inflicted halfway through our journey, in the Gorges of the Loire, a route that promised spectacular vistas at the price of perilous climbs. On one of these climbs I fell, lacking enough momentum to stay upright (I was a lovestruck but halfhearted cyclist). I slid with the bike towards the edge of a gorge, my right side scudding against rocks. Jim dragged me back, showered me with his water bottle, applied every ointment in his first-aid kit, and spackled together the long, deep slice below my elbow. Then he set to fixing the twisted tire. While I watched him sullenly tinker, I was stricken by several ideas. That I had to keep riding, to literally pull my own weight, even if I didn't feel like it. That I was about to yoke myself to someone who had wild notions like this bike trip. That the cut he had crudely and tenderly patched would still be angry and quite visible when I put on The Dress in September.

That I spent weeks fretting about my wound rather than appreciating the man who treated it reveals how young I truly was. I had indeed no business getting married, saddling a good, grown man with such a frivolous girl. But in the end we both went through with it, setting aside our reasonable doubts in favor of our strongest hunches.

Our hunches proved correct. And The Dress, too, was just right for the job. So huge and bright, it created a penumbra around my body that kept even the groom from getting too close; no one even noticed the raw pink scar, not even the photographer. Truth is, The Dress worked far too well. I stepped out of it on my wedding night, revealing to my life's partner the elaborate and sexy architecture beneath—the push-up bra, the hooped slip that put the "ballroom" in the skirt. But he couldn't see—vision impaired, no doubt, by all the top-shelf intoxicants I made my parents pay for. He missed her—the most beautiful woman on earth. But I didn't. I never loved the way I looked again.

Even The Dress itself could not repeat its magic. Seven years later, my husband wrote the script for a low-budget movie featuring a wedding scene. I still had The Dress, so as a cost-cutting measure he and I took the extra roles of bride and groom. I thought it would be a kick, a repeatable thrill, but as I lifted The Dress from the coffin the dry cleaner had packed it in, I was astonished by how heavy it was. And when I accepted the enormous weight on my shoulders and let the taffeta parachute out into the dressing room, its true nature as a costume became viscerally clear; I couldn't believe I had worn such a ponderous garment in my real life. I didn't feel beautiful, I felt ridiculous. I blushed, retroactively embarrassed for myself.

The Dress, in its prodigious breadth and heft, represented everything I did not know about marriage, about anything, really. Appalling the amount of silk, sequins, and tulle needed to disguise my ignorance and console my vanity. I was not, nor have I ever been, the most beautiful woman on earth. I know that now. Back in another cardboard coffin, The Dress will never again be embodied, except, perhaps, if our daughter wants to go to a Halloween party dressed as Princess Di.

But the scar remains, long past anger and fainter each year, and by this adorable wound I ask for the humility it failed at first to teach me. Humbling, this business of coupling for life, of sustaining the body and soul of another. Allow me to remember his face, clenched over the work of keeping the blood inside me. Allow me to look upon it for many more years to come.

By virtue of the wound on my left forearm, I ask to be forgiven for The Dress, to be released at last from the image of me in it and from the monstrous narcissism that called its burden down. By this slender relic of a wound, hidden from the wedding photos but still visible to me, remind me of the true cost of vanity, which is $1200, which I have offered to pay back to my mother, an offer she has repeatedly refused, which is an expression of love as loud as she can make it. Amen.

3. In Honor of the Wound in the Left Breast

August 2016; left breast, above the nipple at 2 o'clock; approximately 1.3 in. long, ¹⁄₁₆ in. wide, ¹⁄₈ in. to ¼ in. deep, depending on severity of lymphedema; appearance of a closed eye, the lash on the fleshy object in the foreground of Dalí's "The Persistence of Memory"; light pink in color; pebbled in texture.

I try not to look at it. I have resisted this wound since the day it was carved by a surgeon's sure hand, resisted discussing it, resisted writing it, resisted running in foot races or eating a magenta bagel or ironically drinking rosé in its honor. I did not celebrate the fifth birthday of the wound, an encouraging milestone that discourages me. I hate the term *survivor*, as if every soul on earth were not in this category.

But this wound knows me, all my postures and evasions. Any glance, however stolen, is met with its conspiratorial wink, deep in the flesh, the vertiginous sensation of seeing and being seen at once. This is the portal through which I dare not enter unless I want to be punished, to confirm my worst suspicion: that I did this to myself. By filtering too little of what passed between me and the poisoned world—air, water, wine, salt. By donning the raiments of sanctioned womanhood—virgin, temptress, nursing mother—and letting them speak for me. By believing in my own divine symmetry.

Beneath the all-seeing closed eye is the scar tissue, invisible until massaged by a lover or a lymphedema therapist or by the one who cravenly aches for the breast to be reborn as an instrument of pleasure. As her fingers meet the seams of cells charred by radiation, she touches the rough bottom of herself, understands the irrevocable, all that withstands persuasion and desire.

By this adorable and disturbing wound—this divot, this trench, this filched pocket of the pudding—I ask permission to avert my gaze a little longer, until Christmas maybe, turtleneck season, until the vision of my own corpse no longer spies me with its little eye. Abjectly and stubbornly, I ask permission to turn this page in the body of the book once more.

And by the way, and by virtue of the wound in the left breast, please stop strafing me with bullets painted pink. I am down, I am on the ground, you can count me among the casualties. By this venerable gouge, wonderous and banal as milk, I beseech you to use your rose-colored benevolence to worship every woman every blessed day, and to get the goddamned toxins out of the fry pans. Amen.

4. In Honor of the Wound in the Abdomen

March 2021; directly beneath the navel; approximately ¾ in. long and ⅛ in. wide; straight vertical line, appearance of an unusually erect earthworm or a bold hashmark in a count of five; mauve in color; slightly ropy in texture.

The womb is a tiny house—size of a pear, size of a clenched fist—and the Christian paradox of the womb is that such a small house can contain God. Mine once housed two gods, performing its miraculous expansion and contraction twice in three years and then never again.

My little house cast out its last dweller in 1995, and my big house, a six-bedroom pile of sooty Pittsburgh bricks and timber, saw that god depart and ascend to a celestial apartment in Washington, D.C. in early 2021. In other words, my nests were empty. And so there was an uncanny harmony in letting go of both of them that spring, undergoing a radical hysterectomy and the selling of our home of 35 years.

My uterus and ovaries, once my body's more reliable appliances, were behaving in ways that troubled my gynecologist, turning vaginal ultrasounds, biopsies, and D&Cs into bleak new hobbies. The house where my husband and I started our marriage and where we raised our children was likewise acting up, changing the nature of our relationship to it. Once it had felt like a conservatory, nurturing the messy flowering of our family life. Now its true nature, stuffy and fragile, revealed itself with alarming frequency. The last unairconditioned private home in America, our permanent address, whose landline number is the only one we'll ever remember, was one burst centenarian pipe away from leveling us. Both houses needed care we were suddenly certain we could no longer give.

It is an indication of my naivete, or more likely the fact that I hadn't moved since 1985, that it didn't occur to me that moving would be so strenuous and that my same-day surgery would require a long period of recuperation, during which I was forbidden to strain at all—no lifting, no engaging of the abdomen for any purpose, lest the incision, neatly stitched like a zipper beneath my navel, unzipped.

Add to this the strain of finding a buyer for an old inner-city house for a price that would cover the cost of the edgy new condo we'd purchased in a renovated church. To meet our number, our real estate agent told us, we would have to "stage" the old joint, which meant clearing all of its closets, cupboards, and surfaces, then placing porcelain bowls, rolled white towels, potted plants, and bottles of San Pellegrino in strategic positions to make it look like the pictures of the new condo we had just been sold.

Irony and anxiety were thick on the ground, then, along with drifts and dunes of objects that needed disposing. Like my surgery, our downsizing was radical—from six bedrooms to two, from a cavernous attic to none, from a full basement and two-car garage to a storage cage and a numbered spot. Virtually everything had to go, and I could not lift any of it, though I could triage and dispatch—which meant telling my husband what to do a thousand times a day, which is roughly one thousand more times than he can tolerate.

Seated cross-legged on the floor, a Buddha with a hot-water bottle across my belly, I mimed serenity while ruthlessly dispossessing us—of dressers, of desks, of filing cabinets, of hope chests, of stained bathrobes and pilled sweaters, of joke mugs and mug-warmers, of milkshake, panini, and fro-yo makers, of coat hangers, pants hangers, wire hangers, of twin beds and double beds and the faded sheets for those beds, of window fans, of perfectly good winter coats (oh look, more hangers), of trial-size cosmetics and splayed nail brushes and 40-year-old tins of VapoRub, of futons, of backup curtain rods and picture frames, of leftover epoxy and the not-for-company towels, of DVDs, albums, CD towers, and cassette coffers, of books, books, books, books, of single mittens and threadbare gloves, of three-ring binders, reinforcement stickers, and semi-desiccated Sharpies, of walk-a-thon t-shirts and ballcaps for teams we no longer rooted for, of pantyhose, of garment bags, vanity bags, tote bags, string bags, monogrammed laundry bags, of brooms (though I know it is unlucky) and shovels and rakes, of candy dishes and candlesticks, of all plastic Christmas ornaments and most of the blue ones, of one light-up snowman and two tangled packages of tinsel.

And that was just the surface debridement. Deep in the flesh of our house, in its rafters and caverns, were crates containing two lifetimes of paper-based correspondence and academic pursuits, were the fat plastic reliquaries of our children's' childhoods—their teeth, their hair, their handprints, footprints, inscrutable scrawls and stick-figure sketches, their lumpen ceramic vessels and crayoned odes, one of which begins:

Mom
Ultra Durable, Loving Warranty
A most charming play toy garuntee
She'll make your bed, she'll feed you bread
She comes with a free Mr. Potatoe Head
She keeps you healthy, she keeps you stealthy
Your automatically fairly wealthy . . .

I'd like to note here that I never made anybody's bed but my own. But sorting through such tender detritus seriously strained not my abdomen but my heart. I lifted nothing and read everything. My adolescent poetry and earnest French compositions. Letters from friends who were *dying* to talk to me, even though they were simply on vacation. The last passionate missive from my last serious boyfriend. A briefcase filled with weird news clippings and raw poems typed on onion skin paper that were the ammunition in my husband's sustained campaign to marry me. The poignant truths tumbling out of the rhyme schemes of babes.

How hard we all took things, it occurred to me now, how wealthy in feeling we once were. And along with that came an understanding that what I was touching for the last time in my sweltering attic were not objects but emotions, yellowed and fading to sentiment in my hands. Some of these treasures I took pictures of, but most everything else I directed my husband (using every synonym imaginable for "please") to toss, not reluctantly but somberly, understanding that they'd exhaled their last warm breaths. Would I ever again need to read them? Would anyone, including me, ever willingly carry them on their backs? Such practical questions revealed clarifying truths: No one, including my children, will want to archive my papers. I have, and have been, deeply loved.

Clearly it was time, not just to move but to move on. It was like figuring out that a religion in which you'd once believed fervently was now just a church, emptied of its saints and songs. And will there ever come another to replace it? Other deities on earth in whom to be in such thrall? I don't know. Perhaps this is the true nature of loss—not of things themselves but of the way we care about things, not of people themselves but of the way they make us feel, not of the body itself but of what the body, once ultra-durable, can endure.

*

Size of a drumstick, weight of a deck of cards, my uterus slipped out of a slit beneath my navel and fell into the capable hands of a woman who then sent it to another woman for dissection. Her lab report begins narratively, "The specimen is received fresh labeled with the patient's name, initials KK," and then devolves into a litany of "gross" observations, which means that they were made with the eyes.

It was through the eyes of Dr. Thing Rinda Soong, M.D., Ph.D., that I finally saw the house of God: *pink-tan and glistening, grossly unremarkable.* Then she goes deeper, slicing through the rose-colored walls, noticing *dystrophic calcifications, cortical inclusion cysts, leiomyoma, adenomyosis, endometriosis*—words that were not images until I looked them up, conjuring a house degraded by time—plaster dinged, shingles loose, gables strangled by ivy. From the clinical expression of Dr. Soong's deep attention, I learned the happy source of my difficulties—age itself, nothing as remarkable as cancer.

Nonetheless, I was overwhelmed, shedding tears over the testimony of this gross observer, this bearer of not-bad news—or maybe I was just stupidly, freakishly tired. I wondered whether my body had ever been handled with such focused consideration as it had by Dr. Soong. Perhaps my mother once touched me in this way, carefully learning the marvelous being that emerged from her sacred house. Her given name, as it happens, is Mary, which she also bestowed upon me, making me Kristin Mary, an inadvertent invocation of the holy incarnation.

By this adorable wound, stigmata of female passion, of heaven and earth finding refuge in a little space, I ask to be reminded of my lucky, cloistered life. Only the womb can contain a god, and only a house can hold a family, not for always but for a time made precious by its fierce and fleeting passions. Remind me not to rue my unimportance. Remind me I, too, was once a god. Remind me I once came with a free Mr. Potato Head.

By this mercifully common and unremarkable wound, I request a firmament, a celestial roof over the heads of my children, now blithely walking the savage streets of Brooklyn and D.C., and a clean set of sheets wherever they lay their heads with whomever they lie with and compose rhapsodic odes to, and two good winter coats because it's cold out there and they couldn't sacrifice even a single day of their spectacular, motherless lives to come and take them off my hands. Amen.

5. In Honor of the Wound in the Left-Hand Pinkie Finger
September 2021; bottom of fifth digit, just above the webbing; approximately ½ in. in length, ⅟₁₆ in. in width; convex in appearance, a contact lens seen from the side, a smile drawn by a small hand; sunrise pink in color; slightly raised and firm in texture.

I was singing, shyly, because our house was a charmless bunker fashioned out of cinder blocks and tile, an acoustic design perfect for broadcasting our blunt American voices to the tiny French village where we were attempting to fit in. I was preparing to spread an avocado on toast and to eat it outside on the terrace, which in my first September after retiring from teaching was a daily hit of nourishing autumnal sun and wish fulfillment. Of course, there was good *pain de campagne*, which I cut, humming, with a terrifically long and toothy knife, perfect for its purpose.

I used the knife again to halve the avocado, engaging only two of its copious teeth, and the fruit broke apart in my palms, *à point*, perfectly ripe. The pit, however, stuck hard in one half, in what the French call *la chair*, or *the flesh* of the fruit. A quick stab and flick of the knife would do the trick, and as I was struggling with this maneuver I saw the tender pink pillow of my palm beneath the flayed avocado, far below my other hand, which was wielding the knife like a sword from the dizzying height of its long blade. As I formulated the thought that this was a dangerous thing to do, the knifepoint slipped on the oily pit and glided into my little finger, slicing its bottom morsel of flesh with the same ease it would have had with the avocado's.

I screamed and dashed to the sink, watched blood bubble up against the feeble pressure of the water. I flushed—a complex, whole-body reflex of pain and shame for having done something so manifestly stupid. Jim ran in from outside, confirming that all of France had heard me, and as I clutched a sponge and lifted my hand far above my head, I looked down at the countertop below to see the avocado half, pit still firmly imbedded, floating pristinely as a tropical island in a sea of my blood.

With bandages rummaged from our bags, Jim frantically mummified the cut, as he had thirty-seven years before in this very country when I fell off my bicycle. We watched, breath held, for seepage, for a clue of what to do next. "I don't want to go to an emergency room," I said firmly, "full of Covid." Though we'd escaped our careers and our country in the receding tide between coronavirus waves, hospitals were still seeing cases. Jim nodded, rewinding his vision from the gash he'd just buried.

We'd never been to a French emergency room, *les urgences*; we didn't even know how to get to one, how to pay for a visit; we hadn't gotten that far in our wildly impractical and improvisational plan to retire and spend some months in France. I felt the first sickening waves of dread, of a bad idea getting worse, batting against the bandages.

There was an unspoken feeling between us that this little accident, should we acknowledge its seriousness, would bring our fantasy life, barely started, to an end. Having just endured two years of constant crisis—dodging disease and enduring the complete upending of our professional lives—we were triggered into remembering how easily the world as you understand it slips out from under you, no matter where you are. We decided to sleep on it, and we drifted into a wishful, troubled slumber, me with my hand above my head and both of us tamping down the fear that I might begin to bleed again. (There is a pill for such fears, and we each took one.) I woke in the morning and my hand still throbbed—reminding me how profound and urgent the wound was—but the bandages had held.

My neighbor Geneviève stopped by to confirm my weekly bread order. Trying to sound offhand while waving my mummified hand, I explained the *petit accident* and asked what she thought I should do. She recommended the pharmacy in the village next to ours that had a drop-in doctor.

The pharmacy! Something that could be handled at the pharmacy could *not* be an emergency! We decided to go there *tout de suite* and made a list of other things we needed (more bandages, and what the hell was the word for *Q tips*?), and while we were at it we made another list for the superstore—the *hypermarché*—in the big town beyond that. There were suddenly many things we needed, along with the words for them in French, including baking powder (*chimique à levure*) for a cake I was now determined to make, printer ink (*encre d'imprimante*) and a fly swatter (*tappette à mouche*) and a salad bowl (*saladier*). We scribbled joyously in our relief that we were officially *not* in an emergency, returning us to the kind of adventure we'd signed on for—the wonderful strangeness of ordinary things elsewhere.

We parted a huddle of smokers to enter the sleek hygienic palace that is every pharmacy in France, sauntering through the homeopathic infusions, anti-aging creams, and jewel-like soaps and perfumes, to the chic lab-coated pharmacist at the counter. Casually, after first asking for the Q-tips, I enquired about having the doctor take a look at my hand, and when I described what I had done, she said I could wait for the doctor outside, gesturing to the smoking scrum, for two hours or more. Should I need stitches, she added, I would need to go to the *urgences*.

It says something about us, about our profound denial of reality or maybe just an aversion to waiting for anything, which is so deep in my husband's temperament that it is reflexively part of mine, too, that we could better imagine moving to another country than we could stopping two hours to have my finger reassembled. We paid for our Q-Tips (*coton-tigues*) and got out of there. Or maybe it says something about the true nature of our problem, which was in the realm above a First World one—a problem of our own making during an experience of great good fortune.

It was a heavenly problem, then, which continued to unfold in the surreal abundance of a French *hypermarché*. We plowed through our list, chucking sponges (*éponges*) and oatmeal (*flocons d'avoine*) and raisins (curiously hard to find in a country covered in grapevines) in the cart. My hand aloft as I steered through the *hectares* of aisles was the only reminder that all was not well, that there were questions not yet asked or answered—*Is* this an emergency? What the hell are we doing here?

Back home, after unloading our bazaar of purchases, Jim and I got down to dealing with my hand. The tourniquet of bandages he'd applied was now firmly embedded in the cut. He watched a YouTube video that recommended soaking them in warm water, which we did in the new *saladier*. After unwinding several layers, black with blood, my pinkie finger appeared murkily under the water, a disturbing, jagged flap of white flesh gaping open below the knuckle. It looked bad, like a malformed specimen in formaldehyde, and the idea of putting the flesh back together revealed itself as a task beyond YouTube.

Still, given the late hour and the probability we'd be hours at the *urgences* and the fact that we had a dinner invitation that evening—a rare opportunity to audition our fantasy life in France with actual French people—we decided that *the next day* would be given over to to repairing the wound, even though we silently agreed it was now, in all likelihood, an emergency. In the meantime, I baked a cake with one hand. I took it to dinner, where our French friends claimed to like it and kept their laughter respectable when I asked for more *boules* (which means *balls*) instead of *bulles* (which means *bubbles*) while the champagne was going around. I drank only a moderate amount (a trick I'd learned from them) but still felt woozy—from disorganized thinking in two languages, from shame (everyone very alarmed by my hand and giving instructions on how to find the *urgences*) and fear (of the *urgences* itself, of explaining my ridiculous accident in my ineloquent French, of the Covid germs waiting for me there, more patient than us).

We woke up very early the next day; I packed water and snacks and books. Despite our friends' detailed instructions, we got lost. The *urgences* was not well marked and could only be entered via a steep, fearsome ramp with no sidewalk, presumably for ambulances. This I mounted alone, like the scaffolding to my ultimate punishment, while Jim looked for parking in the maze of narrow streets around the hospital. Here is the dark side of experiencing ordinary things elsewhere; as hard as you try, you often miss a key detail—like where there is short-term parking—that can quickly torpedo any mission into absurdity and chaos.

The *urgences* was an unadorned, uncomfortably close room with molded plastic chairs and a couple of vending machines. After registering at a gritty window, I sat down and cased out the emergencies ahead of me—three parent-child couples who greeted me politely from behind their masks, as French people do no matter where they encounter you. I wondered whether Jim would find a parking spot or ever find me again without my navigation (though he second-guesses my directions). But after a tense half-hour he appeared, and we settled in with our novels and N95s, shoulder to shoulder, at last in an emergency.

In the waiting room, I had some time to think. In our other life, the one I continued to imagine as our real one, the very things we were now calmly tolerating—being lost and searching for parking and waiting for anything— would have been their own kind of catastrophe. I have been put in the doghouse for choosing the wrong toll-booth line. He's received my seething scorn for making us arrive ten minutes early to a party. That we had come this far, all the way to the *urgences*, without one of us blaming the other for any of the missteps and inconveniences was, well, strange.

This, more than the sight of my own mangled hand, brought the urgency of the situation home to me.

I thought about other moments when the background static of our union, of long marriage and radical proximity, went quiet like this. The births of our children. Their illnesses, one dire for each. My cancer. The morning of his mother's death. I took a deep, filtered inhale of that shocked peace, the oxygen of our lives, both real and imagined.

Before even an hour had passed, I was called back, and a young ponytailed doctor in sneakers unceremoniously dismantled my bandages, soaked my cut in Betadine, and administered a tetanus test. She complimented Jim's rough work but said, *tant pis*, the wound was too old for stitches; I'd waited too long to come to the *urgences*. She wrapped my finger deftly; it would have to heal on its own. She wrote me a script for everything she used to dress the wound and sent me back to the pharmacy with a warm *au revoir*. Sputtering from the rapidity at which all of this transpired, I asked her whom I needed to pay, and she looked at me with amused pity. No one, she said merrily. *C'est une urgence!*

By this crude and adorable wound, tough as a string around my finger, remind me to cut my fruit wearing an oven mitt. By this new wrinkle in my palm, show me that the line between joy and pain is literally a knife's edge, and keep this knowledge awake in me, even when I'm singing my head off.

And throw in universal healthcare, please, a sneakered doctor tending every wound on earth.

By this deeply embarrassing wound, curled in the hammock of skin below my wedding ring, I also request a tomb for my superficial regrets. Sometimes the kind of love that has been my portion—sensible and steadfast and enduring—disappoints me. Disappoints as well those who have paid my outrageous bills and changed my bloody dressings. By virtue of the wound in my left pinky finger, forgive me for missing the counterpoint of disappointment, which is amazement. Allow me to be amazed in the future where love will look a lot like an emergency room—grim work done daily, tenderly, and without bitterness.

*

It is said that as Clare suffered her last mortifications, unable to rise from her bed to attend Christmas mass at the Basilica in Assisi, she miraculously saw the entire ceremony in all its glorious detail projected on the walls of her austere cell. And that is how she became, in addition to founder of the Poor Clares and author of its Rule of Life, the patron saint of sore eyes, embroidery, and television.

And so in her name, and by the fifth and doubtless not last wound, I raise the faithless, damaged left hand to make a final supplication. Even if my eyesight should fail and my memory falter, even if none of my wild demands for mercy are met, let me keep one thing: this vision, revealed in the book of my own bruised body, until the end of my corporeal days. Amen.

Dana Levin

On Robert Hass's "A Story About the Body"

When *Poetry Daily* put out the call for an essay that might "focus on any kind of prose…that has sparked a change in how you approach writing or reading poetry," I thought instantly of two books by philosophers who have offered me enduring lenses: *The Poetics of Space* by Gaston Bachelard and *I and Thou* by Martin Buber. Then I flashed on the bowl of dead bees at the end of Robert Hass's famous poem.

Suddenly, just by *thinking* about Bachelard and Buber, it was as if I could understand Hass's poem wholly and clearly for the very first time. It was the story of a test—at stake was human intimacy. I understood the ways in which the main character fails this test, and how intimacy lends the poem's ending image such expressive power. Intimacy: it was a central subject for my favorite mystic-philosophers, and it was the central subject of "A Story About the Body." For most of the thirty years I'd been reading and teaching this poem, I'd been caught up wholly in the vividness of its figurations; while I understood the plot of the poem, I'd never really stopped to seriously *feel* into its nuances—or how the narrative journey positions its final lyric revelation. Bachelard and Buber helped me read the poem anew.

So: first, the philosophers, then the poem and a writing prompt.

Gaston Bachelard and the Abodes of Consciousness

Gaston Bachelard was a well-known French Philosopher of Science who in older age took a giant left turn and started writing what a lot of other philosophers thought were crazy books, with titles like *The Psychoanalysis of Fire* and *The Poetics of Space*. He is most famous in popular circles for this last, his landmark book on architecture and the poetic image. When I first read this book in college, I had just finished a Literary Criticism class and was feeling jaundiced about it and lit crit in general. Then a new semester began and with it a class called Art and Environment, where *The Poetics of Space* was our only textbook—it changed how I saw the world.

In *The Poetics of Space*, objects and spaces are occasions: they elicit from Bachelard much lyric enthusiasm and casual psychoanalysis, alternating between intellectual swoon and *ce n'est rien, it is nothing*. Here he is waxing poetic in a chapter called "Drawers, Chests, and Wardrobes":

> If we give objects the friendship they should have,
> we do not open a wardrobe without a slight start.
> Beneath its russet wood, a wardrobe is a very white
> almond.

Bachelard's approach to objects marries the outer properties of an object to inner properties: both the empiric (the five sense physicality of a thing) and the oneiric (the dreamy) properties, both the objective and subjective properties: in his phenomenological system, an object cannot be fully known unless we add its associational properties. An object is not a thing as much as a constellation of physical and psychological elements. It is "an abode of consciousness," in the words of architecture historian Joan Ockman.

In some ways, this sounds like a Hippie version of T.S. Eliot's idea of the objective correlative, an idea which has informed modern and contemporary poetics for over a hundred years—you likely know it as "show, don't tell." In 1920's "Hamlet and His Problems," where Eliot first lays out his idea of the objective correlative, he contends that:

> The only way of expressing emotion in the form
> of art is by finding an "objective correlative"; in
> other words, a set of objects, a situation, a chain of
> events which shall be the formula of that particular

emotion; such that when the external facts…are
given, the emotion is immediately evoked…

Eliot makes the object part of the objective correlative sound like, well, an object: a vessel to infuse with feeling in the creation of poetry. I think Bachelard conceives of the relationship between object and psyche a little differently. If I were to draw a schematic of how Eliot describes the process and effect of the objective correlative "formula" versus how Bachelard describes the birth of the poetic image, it might look like this:

Eliot's Objective Correlative:
Poet → Object → Poem

Bachelardian poetics:
Object →   ← Poet
          ↓
      Poem

For Bachelard, the poetic image is the product of object and poet communing; it's relational. An unabashed personifier, Bachelard speaks often in *The Poetics of Space* about objects and intimacy: "Wardrobes with their shelves, desks with their drawers, and chests with their false bottoms are veritable organs of the secret psychological life. Indeed, without these 'objects'…our intimate life would lack a model of intimacy. They are hybrid objects, subject objects. Like us, through us and for us, they have a quality of intimacy."

Martin Buber and Facing Thou

The word *intimacy* has its root in the Latin *intus*: within. To encounter an object with intimacy requires a certain kind of attuned openness, a quality of listening to and respect for the is-ness of the thing before you. Here I come back, as I often do, to 20th-century philosopher Martin Buber, and his book *I and Thou*. In it, Buber says the I engages the Not-I in two primary ways: I-It and I-Thou. I-It emphasizes what an I uses and experiences; I-Thou acknowledges a living relationship. Rather than *experiencing*, I-Thou is about *encountering*:

> If I face a human being as my Thou, and say the
> primary word I-Thou to him, he is not a thing among
> things, and does not consist of things…whole
> in himself, he is Thou and fills the heavens.

True intimacy requires a Thou state of mind, whether we are encountering a person, an animal, a plant, or an object, because I-It obstructs contact with *intus*: what is within. To observe, describe, analyze, and categorize is to take the subject position of the subject-object relationship. I-It is not about developing intimacy, it's about developing mastery and control. I-It is about power.

I-It is also about looking. The thing about things is: we see them and then we want them and then—we take hold. We possess and direct ourselves upon them.

What happens, then, when the object seen and desired is a person? The choice between engaging them as It or as Thou has far-reaching effect, both in the realms of intimacy and in the realms of civic life. Racism, sexism, homo- and trans-phobia, xenophobia: all fester under the pernicious influence of I-It dynamics. Personifying an object is one thing; objectifying a person is quite another.

A Story About the Body
Robert Hass

The young composer, working that summer at an
artist's colony, had watched her for a week. She was

Japanese, a painter, almost sixty, and he thought he was in love with her. He loved her work, and her work was like the way she moved her body, used her hands, looked at him directly when she made amused and considered answers to his questions. One night, walking back from a concert, they came to her door and she turned to him and said, "I think you would like to have me. I would like that too, but I must tell you that I have had a double mastectomy," and when he didn't understand, "I've lost both my breasts." The radiance that he had carried around in his belly and chest cavity—like music—withered very quickly, and he made himself look at her when he said, "I'm sorry. I don't think I could." He walked back to his own cabin through the pines, and in the morning he found a small blue bowl on the porch outside his door. It looked to be full of rose petals, but he found when he picked it up that the rose petals were on top; the rest of the bowl—she must have swept them from the corners of her studio— was full of dead bees.

Looking and wanting, seeing and rejecting, confusing art for artist and artist for art: thus our "young composer." The plot turns on the action of gazing: he "watched her for a week"; she "looked at him directly when she made amused and considered answers to his questions"; and, devastatingly, "he made himself look at her when he said, 'I'm sorry. I don't think I could.'" He's lost in a simile: he loves her work, and her work "was like the way she moved her body, used her hands," her art just a proxy. She is an exotic Other, based on the surfaces that he can see: older, foreign, engaged in a different art form. Her presence, for him, is primarily visual and completely aesthetic. He thinks this means he's in love with her, but really it seems like he's in love with the whole *mise-en-scène* of an art colony, of which she is his object among objects. He's a Pygmalion-in-training enthralled by the Galatea he's built in his mind, but the Japanese painter, unlike in the Greek myth, is no statue: when she reveals her mastectomy after boldly affirming their mutual desire, she's asking him if he wants to see below these surfaces; she invites him *intus*, within, to see if he really wants her to be Thou, a person.

When he doesn't, Hass offers readers one of the more arresting objective correlatives of 20th-century American poetry. Familiarity—the poem remains one of Hass's best known—hasn't yet dulled for me the vivid reflexive light of the final image. "A Story about the Body," which, as a poem, is of course a made object, becomes, by its end, a kind of infinity mirror: those structures made of parallel mirrors which create a series of smaller and smaller reflections that appear to recede into infinite distance. You can experience this effect by visiting the fantastic installations made by Japanese artist Yayoi Kusama, or certain kinds of dressing rooms, bathrooms, or halls of mirrors: anywhere you can stand between two mirrors facing each other—and "two mirrors facing each other" sounds like a pretty good metaphor for what happens when, as in this poem, two people are negotiating intimacy.

By the end of "A Story about the Body," we encounter a made object (the poem) that resolves around a made object (the ending image) that presents a made object (the bowl of bees) that binds aptness, physicality, and emotive resonance into a made object: an emblem. Receiving the fullness of this emblem depends on tapping into a Bachelardian state of mind: one that can encounter the bowl of dead bees not as an inert vessel but as an abode of consciousness. Inert vessel vs. abode of consciousness: this is the very choice the Japanese painter poses to the young composer, when she reveals herself not as It, but as Thou.

The bowl she fills in the wake of his failure is an artifact fused with hurt and irony. The rose petals—perennial symbols of love and romance—obscure a collection of dead pollinators: no honey is about to be made by this meeting of flower and bee, at this hive of an art colony. As with most arresting images, the arrival of the bowl re-angles how

I consider parts of the poem already read: in this case, setting, which is now made ironic: art colonies intend cross-pollination, fertilization, and bloom, not sting and death. The bowl of rose-covered dead bees is a clear, precise expression of rebuke delivered straight to the composer's front door: intimate and elegant, a painter's speech-without-saying.

—

Writing Prompt:

Find an object in the world, in memory, or in dream, that made some kind of impression on you. Free-write on its physical properties, and then commune with it in a Bachelardian way: how does it make you feel? What does it make you think about or remember? Generate as much raw material as you can and let associations proliferate. Then write a draft that tells the story of your encounter with this object. *Poetry Daily* asked me to provide an example from my own work of a poem written in this manner, and so I offer up a recent one, which began as a meditation on spindles: "A Walk in the Park" (https://www. southeastreview.org/single-post/poetry-by-dana-levin).

Originally published in Poetry Daily

Minadora Macheret

Grief-Keeping

1. The first prayer I remember was shma ysrael Adonai elohaynu… trailing off into quiet murmurings of twitching lips, children's hands covering their eyes as they recited the rest of the prayer. Too holy of a moment, in case God decided to appear. *You cover your eyes to concentrate,* the rabbi reminds us.

2. Australian raptors carry burning twigs and tree sediment to flush out their prey. I keep misspelling prey as pray. Suppose raptors pray. They ask the forest for mice and voles. They whistle or make a hoarse scream, a holy echo, a trance for their prey to follow. Scientists once believed only humans and lightning could control (perhaps create) fire. Raptors remember fire as a burnt offering.

3. Once, as everyone recited their devotion to God, I peeked through the slits of my splayed fingers and saw: the bimah with the rabbi peering into his hands, the ark, with its gold and silk covering, open, cradling holy scrolls, the rows of cheap foldable seats, the gum a child stuck to the seat cover, the classmates not wanting to participate staring down at their shoes.

4. Another rabbi says, *you cover your eyes because how can you have complete faith in God,*

with all the pain around

us?

5. The first time the basement flooded, my father ran to the closet filled with suitcases of my mother's clothing and wept. Beige in color, now a deep-wet clay with black embroidering of her initials, N.M. The water filling the knitting of her clothing, the silk dresses, the scarves full of animals and bright, sunset colors. An offering he never meant to give.

6. I have a tendency to read warning labels and look up the common side effects of medications obsessively. I never know how my body will react to a moment much less a series of chemicals. We are only chemicals; my best friend reminds me.

7. When there is a sudden loss of a person or a long-term separation, scientists have found a chemical for grief: corticotropin. It floods the system, a sibling of cortisol, and lights up neural pathways predetermined for depression in the brain.

8. The first time I heard you are not enough, it must have started a chain reaction, a beginning of corticotropin to bubble in the brain.

9. The first time my mother prayed, or rather, that I remember, was for shabbat six months before she passed. Two candles in blue and silver ceramic holders. A silk tallit wrapped around her face like a shawl, her hands covering her eyes, as she mouths the words to welcome shabbat. The candles flicker. I've always lingered on this memory. How women call in shabbat. How women call in God, call in the light— as a way of making up for Eve's sin.

10. How she hoped this was enough.

11. In Judaism, so much has burned—from books to people to the bush with all its holiness—even offerings left with a smolder and an ache.

This grief a burning line through our lineage, a forest caught unaware, as the underbrush blazes.

12. Hunters or nature enthusiasts use a bird-blind to watch the natural world in action. A tiny slit across metal or wood, like openings in my splayed fingers, offers freedom into a space consumed by bears and voles and foxes, scuttling across the foliage. On occasion birds will land mere feet from the looker. If they are super lucky, a raptor will perch and preen, eyes alert for its next meal, always surveying the topography.

13. When raptors are kept as pets or caught in the wild, blinders are placed over their eyes. For their own protection. To make them think they're safe. Much like the rabbi who thinks we're safe when we close our eyes.

14. In a leather jacket from the 1970s I inherited from my mother; I found a folded-up sheet of paper. On it she wrote affirmations or maybe reminders or tiny prayers:

> *I am smart enough*
>
> *I am good enough*
>
> *I am pretty enough*

15. If I could name grief, I would call it a jacket, too big for your body. Constantly squirming, trying to wriggle into or out of, fully encapsulated. I am lost in the smell of her perfume and leather. I stand in front of the mirror, my face an angle between slats, the space between prayer fingers. My face her silhouette, slipping.

Originally published in *Brevity*

Ray Malone

Cinder 136

Wakes, walks to the window, inches
from the pane, breathes out, long breath
bearing its mist, mist appears, pale,
first finger writes a name, stares at,
sees through same to the world below,
world it forms, figures, as the name
fades from the pane, breathes in again,
inches away from the window,
world remains, other world remains

Originally published in Star 82 Review

Mary B. Moore

The Teachings of Naranja

My beloved is the grandson
of Naranja, the spiritual teacher

whose sayings I never hear
in the dream, but his wife, bearer of wisdom's

bed-weight, a crone whose round tan face
earth has freckled umber,

sits at the small pine
table. Its labors have warped it—

bearing meals, talk, elbows,
heads pondering sorrow.

She asks if I'm interested
in her or Naranja.

Both/and I think.
My beloved who also

sits at the table spoons
thick spicy soup, pumpkin perhaps,

shaking out pepper and salt,
black and white pigments, swaths,

dots and lines, a sand-painting
he will eat,

a hot communion.
I wake to remembering

naranja is Spanish for *orange*, which
the unconscious

made soup of. I say "the"
because clearly I'm not in charge.

Oranges are. They lit
the polished deep green leaves,

the groves' fragrant shadows
that beckoned girl-me,

who ate so much
juice, fire and sugar:

The sun fed orange. Color tells.
Black and white, the ground

salt and pepper—
oh, I know my Jung—

binaries, self and soul, crone
and beloved—but the ground

is the word
arising, the unwarranted love

the earth we are
burning gives

the blossoming
scent of oranges

I peel and eat over the sink.
The teacher is burning.

Originally published in Birmingham Poetry Review

Marilyn Moriarty

Bone Lab

> *No ideas but in things.*
> —**William Carlos Williams,** *Paterson*

Someone was murdered in the pay-lot the day before I interviewed for the job teaching English as a Second Language to foreign students in Los Angeles. I had moved to L.A. to be with my fiancé. Hired, I became the expert in the present tense. My exercises focused on "to be" and "to have." Taught *yes* or *no* questions by inverting syntax. We eventually got to the present continuous which could be used as a future tense. "I am going to take the bus. You are going to drive. She is going to fix the flat. I am going to volunteer at UCLA."

Immersed in the completed past, the Bone Lab was my haven, a quiet place in a basement on the university campus, filled with ancient bones, pottery, and teeth. Glen, an early forties outdoor guy, salt-and-pepper whiskers scraggly like a test-tube brush, taught the graduate night class in anthropology. He had invited night-school students to volunteer in the archaeology lab. Since I always wanted to be an archaeologist, I took the bus across town from my downtown teaching gig to volunteer once a week before class.

"You painted the whole bone," Glen said.

"It's dry now," I said.

"It's the *whole* bone."

I knew that. The proper procedure was to place two vertical lines over a horizontal one on the bone. All the strokes were color-coded, keyed to places in the pueblo. Two vertical lines might indicate the floor and the room where the item was found. A horizontal line under the verticals identified the building. Something like that. The lines were meant to be small, like a footnote number.

Glen's mustache met his beard on the intake to hold in what would soon be a huge explosive laugh.

Elsie, an older woman grad-student with tight gray curls that reminded me of ammonites, was working on her doctorate. Seated at the table, she peered through the window-pane frame of her bi-focals at my bone. Two sets of eyes—hers and Glenn's—stared at my handiwork.

Yes, it was the whole thing.

The bone had *wanted* to be recognized. Its undulating surface, triangular shape like a bike saddle with its points curving upward, called for color. Two vertical strokes and one horizontal--yes. Each horn of the triangle embraced a vivid hue: green, yellow, and red. Even if the style obliterated the orientation of lines, the color brought life to the bone. A tricorn bone. A talisman, a charm, something powerful.

But maybe someone would not be able to link it to its place on the archaeological site where it emerged. "You can't tell which line is on the bottom," Glenn said.

It wasn't a compliment.

"I have another job for you." In one hand a box of tiny bones. "Prairie dog leg bones," he said. "Could you separate the femurs from the tibias?"

He meant: could you separate art from science, spirit from matter?

I emptied the box on the lab table. The bones fell in small piles like matches. Tiny, perfect, but dusty. They had been found on the ground floor of a pueblo or in its midden, trash pile. I suppose the archaeologists were trying to determine what the people ate, these little bones part of a large meal. Now they resembled bows for tiny cellos. It took longer than you might think to separate femurs from tibias. I lined them up on the lab surface to make a progression from smallest to largest, like a representation of human evolution in which a humanoid figure scales up from a knuckle-dragging, comma-backed primate to an upright, striding human, *Homo erectus.* The *erectus* part was important. Bipedal, yes. Erect stature, yes. The hole in the base of the skull could tell us how the head was attached. If the hole was under the skull, the head balanced on the spine—human. Back of the skull, like a cat—the creature walked on four legs.

It was left to someone else to tell the story of this progression. I deposited the bones in a case like a pillbox before I took the bus home.

Chastened and corrected, in the Bone Lab, I embraced the folly of a zen-like apprenticeship requiring me to follow the *sensei's* instructions: cut wood, draw water, line up bones. At some point enlightenment should arrive; awaiting enlightenment, I was grateful for a job so I could hang around the Lab. Any menial task on my volunteer day made me happy. I liked being around calm people, guided by a sense of purpose, who could work with ancient things. Focus like this, I am sure, keeps the earth spinning. Like monks chanting around the clock, like nuns telling their beads, this focused attention created a mindful virtue. Of course, other people's work assignments meant I would not have to think too much about the state of my own life, which was slowly coming to view as it came apart.

*

In ancient times, people speculated about the origin of fossils, but they did not know how minerals replaced organic matter; how softest muscle or even stomach contents can be preserved as the ground leaches out minerals and replaces them. Flesh becomes rock; metal becomes dust.

Aristotle thought fishes swam into their fossil form, finning into narrowing tunnels that trapped them. Stones in the form of shellfish made other ancients wonder if they were produced by a latent power in the earth that grew them. Still others thought shellfish and plants were put in place by a flood and filled with petrifying juices that turned them into stones.

Spontaneous generation! Light rays penetrated the ground. Hard granite mated with the sun. For jewels, let starlight touch earth. Just as flowers like roses and tulips decorated the surface of the earth, fossils decorated its inside, growing and animated by a spark of life no one understood. After the rise of the west and Christian culture, some fossils were explained as being left over by the Great Deluge. But this created a problem: since *Genesis* put the creation of the earth before plants, fowl, fish, and animals, how was it possible that living things could be contained in the earth's crust when they weren't made yet?

Some writers recognized fossils were the remains of living things that had been embedded in the earth. The eighteenth-century comparative anatomist, George Cuvier, marked the birth of paleontology when he understood fossils to be the remains of no-longer living things—and not contemporary animals. Comparing the bones of living African elephants with the elephant bones dug out of the Paris ground, he deduced they were different species. Species could die out; new ones could emerge. Gaps in the fossil record were caused by sudden, violent events that changed the way life evolved and geological layers laid down. Cuvier came up with the earth-shattering theory: catastrophism. Change came fast. It was not gradual over time.

*

Obviously, my creativity was longing to escape in the Bone Lab. I had a job but not a vocation. I had had a fiancé but not a love. I was trying to fit my growing self into the pre-cut holes society had made for me. I had followed the plot of growing up. Find a job. Find a spouse. Ease parents from the burden of raising an adult child. Time to grow up and get out of the house. I did all that. And something still wasn't working, something that wanted to come out in a sunburst of color in a university basement. Bones were pulling it out of me. Glen and Elsie gave guard rails, allowing my stumbling path through the bones as long as I didn't damage any finds.

Still working in the Bone Lab and teaching ESL, I signed up for a canoe trip through UCLA extension. By then, my fiancé and I had broken up, and I was looking for things to do like paddle the Colorado River into Lake Havasu. Three nights of camping. Tents.

First time out, I was an able paddler in my khaki shorts and camp shirt. My canoe partner was a taciturn professional on this trip alone, like me, and not very happy to paddle with me. We didn't talk much. I kept the canoe rhythm. Sweep. Jay. Sweep. Jay. We paddled through canyons cut into red sandstone, steep walls on either side. We paddled through desert where green things sprouted an inch-wide strip by the river, and only dirt beyond. Near the end of our trip, we were going to pass through a Native American reservation. There was a special spot our guide wanted us to see where petroglyphs had been etched in a wall.

We pulled the canoes up onto a sandy bank and took a short hike on a trail skirting a hill. Dry and dusty path. Dull brown of desert earth, shiny brown of the river, now reflecting the dimming night. Polished pebbles on the shore.

On the face of the hill were glyphs. Some linear, some circular. Deliberate drawings signifying. The past was reaching out to us. My eye drew to small things in the dirt at the base of the glyphs. Not pebbles but pebble size. I scooped up some dirt with the hard pellets in them, knotted them in my bandana, and placed it in the pocket of my camp shirt. I thought of them as an offering to the gods of the place. Something left behind as a token, as if a worshipper had wanted to be remembered there.

When we passed through rapids after that, I focused on keeping my knotted-up bandana safe. Like an easy walking horse, the canoe shifted beneath me, rolling side to side balanced by the stroke of my paddle. My find made a hard place against my heart, and my chest warmed it till it became a part of me. I could not wait to bring these fragments back to the Bone Lab and ask Glen what they were.

Later in the week I sat on the sticky bus seat from my place of work in downtown L.A, to UCLA, watching the evolution of money through the window. Buildings changed from steaming sidewalks, liquor stores, and fortune tellers to the high-rise structures, all plate glass and steel, the green lawn of parks, and eventually my favorite place, the La Brea Tar Pits in Hancock Park. The Tar Pits were shallow asphalt pools that trapped finds as old as 38,000 years. On the green baize lawn around a pool of tar, a tableau of mammoths portrayed a heart-breaking story. One full-grown fiberglass, true-to- scale mammoth was frozen in a struggle, buried to its chest in the tar, trunk upraised, trumpeting a call for help. The other adult and the youngster watched from the grassy bank, feet firmly planted at the edge of the tar pit, as the mother (or father) sank in the tar. The mammoths made a nuclear family. I always thought of them as a holy family. A sign nearby points out the mammoths usually traveled in matriarchal groups. The mammoths offer a human tragedy, a sleight of hand creating pathos for our kind in the disguise of the animal. Pathos tracks the plot of evolution.

Studying the tableau through the dirty window in the bus and the apertures in the fence, I touched my pocket to reassure myself I still had my finds.

Extinction event—the animal story in fiberglass.

Inside the museum a movie about the history of the Tar Pits would be running at regular intervals. Small horses got trapped in the tar. Saber-toothed cats leapt upon the horses; the cats became trapped in tar on the horses. Vultures dropped on carcasses and stuck to the cat that was stuck to the horse. Eventually the conglomerate rotted, the bones were stripped under a prehistoric sun, and the pile sank to the bottom until thousands of years later, modern contractors and engineers pulled them out in chunks, teased apart the bones with delicate chisels, matched like to like, sorted the equine fibulas from avian wings, rewired the bones, and all the original distinctions between beast and bird were restored. This place place converted time into space, showed eons of history stacked in pancaked animal remains.

Though my own life had crumbled, I was putting it back together like those people in the museum, an archaeologist restoring original distinctions.

The bus pulled into the half-moon bus stop lot, and I jumped down the steps, trotting in the late afternoon to my session in the bone lab. I could hardly wait to tell Glenn and Elsie.

"Let's see what you found," Glenn said. I unwrapped the knot in my bandana and shook the contents on to the lab. Glenn had only two words for my find. Words fired like missiles from an explosive burst of laughter —not a ha-ha titter or a muffled chuckle, but a laugh deep and full, like riverine turbulence over rocks, like Niagara Falls, this discharge from a grown man's lungs.

The laugh rolled out the red carpet for two words: "Rat turds."

"Coprolites," I thought. There we go. Easy to debunk me. Sure, I was disgusted by the "rocks." But these were hard and desiccated. If I found them inside the boundaries of a dug site, framed by strings tied to sticks in a grid pattern, dug earth in mounds outside the hole, they would have been considered data, evidence of something. If anthropologists were interested in what went into a meal (like prairie dogs), I found what came out. It's easy to believe in nothing. Anyone can destroy a thing. It's harder to make a thing. So, yes! Rat turds!

(They already thought I was an idiot in the Bone Lab. I am thankful for those who suffer fools.)

The medieval monk Erasmus (1466–1536) celebrated fools in his book *The Praise of Folly*. Narrated by a fool through a female persona, *Folly* was so irreverent, it became the first banned book. Taking on the idea that humility takes a soul where a crown cannot, Erasmus changes the meaning—and the valence—of the word "fool," making it synonymous with "blessed." He eventually portrayed Christ as the biggest fool of all, with the cross his greatest folly. Catholic clerics did not appreciate his humor; the Spanish Inquisition burned the book's translators at the stake. Erasmus celebrated the blindness required for love—to see beauty in a lover's mole or a baby's diaper. Or even ourselves. Surely, we must be a fool to see our 5:00 am face in the mirror as something to love. A man who believes his cheating wife is faithful might be more mad than a man who sees a woman in a pumpkin.

Life is full of excrement, even in sacred places, especially in places you love.

*

John Donne, "Meditation IV: The doctor is sent for."

If all the veins in our bodies were extended to rivers, and all the sinews to veins of mines, and all the muscles that lie upon one another, to hills, and all the bones to quarries of stones, and all the other pieces to the proportion of those which correspond to them in the world, the air would be too little for this orb of man to move in, the firmament would be but enough for this star; for, as the whole world hath nothing, to which something in man doth not answer, so hath man many pieces of which the whole world hath no representation.

Our body's bones parallel the earth's quarries says John Donne in his Fourth Meditation; this comparison intending to measure the world against man leads to the idea man exceeds it. Yet it is the earth that invites us back. Bones laid to rest in the ground define a new or restored homeland. Moses, we read in the Old Testament, took Joseph's bones with him in the exodus. Joseph had "straitly sworn the children of Israel, saying, God will surely visit you; and ye shall carry up my bones away hence with you."

Two years after a colleague and professor of Spanish passed away, a procession of friends in the new millennium made our way on the road to the Compostela de Santiago to scatter his bone ashes in Spain. The Compostela was the pilgrim's road to the shrine of Saint James, but our trip was shorter, into the mountains of Frigiliana to walk a tributary of dust.

We marked the way with special medallions on the trail, like those golden markers set out for pilgrims on the path north. Nailed on trees, they marked the dusty trail where we had been ferried from Malaga. On the medallions, a horse, an Andalusian mare and our friend's spirit animal, looked as if she had just jumped from a frieze on the Parthenon, beauteous as a visiting god in disguise, planted in Frigiliana to test mortals on their discernment. When he was alive and living in Malaga, our friend, Dan, washed the Canastera, soaping her with his hands as if the body's braille welded heaven and earth. A horse illuminated our secular pilgrims' path.

On the edge of a dried creek bed, we gathered in a loose circle. Jay, his brother, opened his container with Dan's ashes, poured them out into the dirt.

Dan's particulate body floated in the air and then dropped. This was spreading the ashes. They were not ashes.

I saw it. In a flutter of dust, a piece of bone. Just a sliver. A white fragment. This thing in the dirt came from inside my best friend. It was smaller than a ground squirrel femur. Too small to paint. Not a fossil. No calcium had been replaced by clay or iron or some inert mineral. A piece of the inside that came outside.

White. Never having been in sun or air but decades inside the wet goo of a human body. A bone outside the bone lab. With the deep sadness of its death attached.

I never read *Archaeology* magazine the same way. Images of mummies turn my stomach. Ditto: graves, death furniture, nutrition for the afterlife. Victorians used ground mummy as an ingredient in health food remedies. When *National Geographic* showed the mummy of King Tut, I saw the body degraded, taken apart. There are museums to look at the thousand-years-dead, blackened bodies with protruding teeth and holes for eyes. Bones teach much about the dead but nothing about death itself.

*

"Did you put the bone back?" I asked the brain surgeon. An emergency craniotomy saved my life. For six weeks I remained in denial about having a hole in my skull. A swimmer, I imagined swamping my brain with a dive in the pool. *Glug glug* inside the skull. To correct, I imagined my skull as a tree trunk with a little door cut into it, like a hobbit house. Open and shut the door. Like the adverts for Keebler's bakeshop: my skull had a round, wooden door in a tree, and, inside the tree, elves were making chocolate chip cookies.

"I couldn't," the surgeon said. "Your brain was too swollen. It would have taken more time." The surgery took nine hours, just to get most of the tumor out and untangle it from the brain stem. Even if it wasn't cancer, it was large, like an oversize sofa in a small apartment pushing other furniture to the wall. It took me two years to ask, "How big was that hole?

The images I had seen of my skull showed a cross-section, so the patch appeared simply as a line drawn from one side of the skull to another. A different angle and the surgical reports made me reckon it was the size of my palm. Five screws held a titanium mesh in place. To hold my brain in place.

"Can I still scuba dive?" I asked. Would ocean pressure force my brain out the mesh like a sieve? Under water, would my brain shrink and expand like an accordion? As no answer was forthcoming, it seemed best not to test it.

Before surgery, I thought about scenes from *Hannibal,* when Antony Hopkins dines on Ray Liotta's exposed brain as Liotta talks.

I wanted my bone back.

Osteoporosis does not affect the skull, otherwise my holey skull would have been flimsy as eggshell. I wondered where they put the bone, if it was tossed in a midden to be discovered later by archaeologists and later painted madly by an incompetent grad student. If incinerated, would my titanium mesh end up as metal slag on a conveyor belt?

"Did the mesh extend to the foramen magnum?"—that hole in the bottom of the skull that proved I was not a cat. "It came to the edge," my surgeon said. He reached behind my ear. "You can feel a screw here."

I spent time looking at Mayan trepanned skulls. Sometimes a piece of turquoise made the patch. The turquoise must have been put in after death. I found relief in that. My painted Bone-Lab bone has come full circle. Perhaps even the creativity that wanted to come out in painting the bone has now exploded a place in my head.

"If you have a seen a brain at all, you have only seen dead ones," writes the fairy narrator in "What We Did for Love," a modern fairy tale by Michael Cunningham in the *New York Times Style* Magazine. But a living brain, lit up on the inside, shoots "little geysers of radiance, which run from pure white to scarlet to cobalt." Almost too bright to look at, it radiates like "a miniature sun." A living brain is like an octopus, continues the narrator, quite different from the calamari of a dissected one. I held on to the image of the brain from this story, a living, lighting entity.

Surely the surgery, in removing the tumor, left a space where it had been. "Go home," I told my brain, which I started to think of as a displaced entity I wanted to befriend. While my normal appearance and ability to speak invited friends to check on me, my brain could only do one thing at a time. My French companion, Bernard, intercepted concerned phone calls and explained my reticence. "It is a brain not a leg. It takes time. She has to swim where she belongs."

Mentally I searched for images to picture my brain, hoping to give it help from the inside. I imagined it as a whale shark, but not for long. Too big, square, and patterned with right angles. Better as a dolphin, its arched back rising out of waves, echoing the surgery video on You-tube where the brain wiggles in its bloody jello.

Better still, my brain was a reef creature, bioluminescent, whose flickering lights resolved into a glow. A beam. A beacon. At home in whatever shelter there was. Even if there was metal mesh for a door.

*

The Bone Lab has grown older. It started life in 1973 but became part of a named center in 1989, the Cotsen Institute. Now it is a place written in caps with a tail of associated departments and donors. People come from miles around just to work and research there. What can be has been digitized, but the claim that is still possible to get hands-on experience banners their website.

I don't know if there was a sense of the sacred when I was there in the mid-seventies, maybe only what I brought to the place. When I think of Glenn now, I picture him on a roan horse with a western saddle riding through the desert into the sunset. I see him from the rear, the round haunches of the horse, the brim of his hat, the back of his trail-dusty covered stirrups. He twists in the saddle, one hand on the cantle, and waves. Elsie might have been a grandmother then. Both of them are probably dead now. Maybe even bones.

We start with bones and we end with bones. Our consciousness inhabits them. They grow within to defy gravity. Age hollows them.

Milk feeds them. Workouts build them. Smoking drains them. They are not like rocks or stones. We study them to read their grain of time. We paint them, we analyze them, we burn them, we bury them, and then we dig them up. We add our time to their time. We venerate them. We examine them. Like radio receivers, they link us to the greater, invisible world. Sign and symbol, they both embody and substitute meaning. They abide. They are left over. They remain. When we do not.

*

I did not know about stars or Aristotle or Cuvier when my sixteen-year-old self tied my tennis shoes, knotted a whipcord jacket over my shoulders, and went to the house of Frances and Roy Smith, an older couple with a high-school son my age. Frances worked with me side-by-side at a dress shop in Jacksonville where we were both cashiers. She had invited me over to see what her husband, an amateur paleontologist, brought home. In a musty house like the inside of a clock, jars filled the kitchen cupboard. A jar for sharks' teeth, one for skate (or ray) mouth pieces, one for turtle shell and bones. A small jar for early horse teeth. In the largest jar, and the last to be shown, fossil mammoth teeth. "No ideas but in things," writes William Carlos Williams in *Paterson*. We met time contained in the jars, from all periods of life before writing recorded history.

Under Florida's eastern shore, a fossil layer lay buried; wave action continually eroded it and left deposits on the beach, where Roy went frequently to search. Especially after a hurricane, he rushed to make high tide at the crack of dawn. A tall, thin man, hollow-eyed, skin stretched tight over his skull and squaring his head, he still smoked. He invited me to search with him on a day after a storm.

"Look for the things that are black," Roy instructed. "Anything black on the beach most likely will be a fossil."

Around us stretched a vast expanse of sea. Dull gray clouds curved over us though a crescent of light glinted far out to sea. Crackling electricity in bursts of lighting raised hair on the back of my neck. I waded at the seaside to look in the sand peeled back by the waves. Roy went the opposite direction to the sifty, light dunes that humped around the roots of sea oats. My surf-line footprints filled with water. I spotted something black half-buried in the sand. It looked like a smooth stone, inwardly curling like a conch but not a shell. The inner ear bone of a whale. I shook sand off. I put it in my pocket. Roy eventually called me up to a sandy hillock to see what he had found. A large black tooth. Square and blocky with striations woven in the top like a triple decker sandwich. Mammoth or mastodon.

Sometimes, when I teach excerpts from Kant's *Critique of Judgment*, I pass the ear bone around the class. It is a dull-metallic black and fits into a cupped hand. Its technical name, cochlea, refers to a spiral. Its infolding form resembles a shell.

"Is this beautiful?" I ask.

"What is it?" one will invariably ask.

"How does it feel?" I counter. "Hold it."

Someone will guess a shell, or a rock, or a piece of metal. They will press for identification of the object in the same way they want to know the author of a poem or story.

"You don't need to know what a thing is to see the form in it," I say.

"Purposiveness without a purpose," Kant calls it, the meaningful form found through patterns in nature and the arts. The intellectual recognition of identity or purpose differs from the feeling of beauty. Both the beautiful and the sublime create pathways to the divine. The beautiful produces feelings of harmony and the furthering of the life force. The sublime jars, creating a dissonance that sends us back to our own rationality.

Sometimes, privately, I am tempted to mock Kant's precise but clunky language that reads like German even in translation. Such ironic mockery offers a form of higher praise. I joke Kant to balance awe and respect. Fear of God, Kant would tell us, creates respect; it is not the same thing as being afraid of God.

Kant says nothing about God's sense of humor, to my knowledge. Erasmus knew God loves a fool.

Roy passed away not too long after this. From that morning on the beach, I came to see the place where the world bent double, to walk the edge where land was once sea, where sea was once sky, where sky left its record of light in sediment beneath our feet. Where a bone can be a tool or a body or a piece of art. The body builds its frame; the world takes it apart. We put it back together. This is the story of life.

No better time than after a storm—or just before—to search for what came up.

--

NOTE: Some information about fossils originates in Frank Dawson Adams, *The Birth and Development of the Geologic Sciences* (New York: Dover Books, 1954), "Figured Stones and the Birth of Paleontology," pp. 250–262; and, on rocks, "Generation of Stones," pp. 78–94.

Originally pubished in Dappled Things

Kylan Rice

A Homily

The uncut copse of pine at furthest edge of field turns
        prism as the shadow of a hawk strikes
through its loose-grouped canopy in intermittent
        scanning shafts of splintered noon. The circle's
path refracts. Songbirds
        waver on the lines of wire strung nearby above
the field's perimeter, where I have stopped to stand
        and watch, relearning
what it means to come with nothing to a threshold
        that I hadn't known before was there, made to feel,
as in a dream of being late or naked or of being naked
        and late at the same
time, my total lack of preparation, trying then, in that moment,
        to remember words I know I know so as
to join in the singing, this song
        of mutual appraisal, watchfulness, appetition,
striving and stricken, harmlessness
        transmuting into something like harm, this field
of harm, yet tenderer or more
        indifferent to risk at least. I am, I realize,
the flaw in the prism, where neither sun
        nor shadow pierces through, a knot or node, a nude
of piercelessness that Christ
        has shown can be undone. The body
rendered priceless with its wound, its openness
        to entrance, daylight, thorn
of hawk, thorn
        the bluebird is, the blush
of red along its breast that signifies
        a knowledge of its nakedness, that nervous

Kylan Rice

song it sings while turning on its high
       -strung line in sight
of what desires it, and tilts in flight to zero in.

Originally published in Brink Literary Journal

Kylan Rice

Night Drive

Pond sound, early spring, or is it still late
       winter, still too soon to surge without some risk
into a chorus in the muddy cut
       beneath the bridge that shields
the preexisting watershed, the tenderness each March
       of bittercress, the hooded flag an iris is, this
sudden ample rioting of voice in dark that opens
       as I drive toward you,
then shuts
       like a glimpse, if not into another life, then near
-futurity, the future fraying through, as if the present were already
       an archaic linen that no skin
had felt or known itself as nakedness beneath for years. All winter,

       the word "cost" had sustained me
as a name, less for a method, than a slow laying-claim
       to the only way of thinking
that was mine: compression, then the ravenous
       expenditure of energy in single, wasting bursts,
followed by brittle phases of aimless reconstruction,
       as of hearing in the aftermath of detonation,
white ringing
       rosettes that compensate for their own frailty
with complexity, which protects by inviting
       a hushed, answeringly delicate attention
to the budded detail dense
       and bolting in the narrow compass of a crown
of hemlock-parsley as it blooms
       like sound returning to a pond in spring. What returns

is not so much
       desire, for you

or anyone, as much
      as what desire disallows: the world
for its own sake, how it bursts
      like silence in, like being listened to, the sudden quietness
that I would cause were I to stop and wade into the reeds instead
      of driving west toward you, overshooting
the small ear song is
      pooling in the vernal dark, hurrying the way a sentence
moves if not toward clarity, then at least a feeling
      of having finally arrived, somehow convinced
that this, this end, the end

      of us, was what I knew we'd come to all along.

Originally published in Brink Literary Journal

Matthue Roth

The Shammes

They called him Zaidy, although he was as unlikely to be a grandfather as a father. But the children flocked to him, when there were children. He had a way about him, a simplicity, that made him a bit childlike himself. He spoke clearly, with loud spaces between each word, as though he were always selecting the next one with care and deliberation. By the time he was permitted to leave the assisted-care facility and live on his own, his face had grown wisdom folds and his hair had salt-and-peppered—he was the shining star of the program, and everyone was so proud of him; the director, in bidding him farewell, used the word *valedictorian*. Upon hearing it, he nodded severely and received the compliment with his characteristic modesty; one of the aides helped him look up the word later. He'd learned how to cover up so people didn't realize he was slow, not until they knew him well. Most of the time, they thought he was a sage.

He moved to Manhattan Beach, near a set of cousins. They owned a block of apartments in a brownstone building with a kosher bakery on the first floor. He was adamant about living alone—now that he could, he *would*—and the cousins took mercy on him, gave him a small apartment for next to nothing, and made a match with a job in that downstairs bakery so he could pay for it. He worked there nine years, learning from the baker and the cashiers and the customers, and most of all from the children. He sneaked them broken cookies for free and tied bracelets on their wrists with candy-cane-striped ribbon.

And people liked him. The community cared for him like a family. Not a Shabbos went by when he wasn't invited to a dinner table after prayers on Friday evening, and somebody else for Saturday lunch, and a weekday visit from some mother or another—he addressed them all as *ma'am*—just to make sure his pantry was stocked and the milk in his refrigerator was unspoiled. At synagogue he was the candy man, the arbiter of suckers and lollies and chews.

When the bakery closed its doors (business wasn't what it used to be, and it was sold to the gentiles and reopened as a store for exotic cakes), the community found him another job, at the butcher shop. And when the butcher shop closed (there were no longer enough people living in the neighborhood to sustain it), he was hired by the synagogue.

In terms of a place of employment, the synagogue was both safe and steady. As long as there were people to keep attending, it would continue to exist. And as long as it existed, it would require someone to replace the books on their faltering shelves, to sweep and mop the floor, to unlock the door for the congregants in the morning, to field maintenance requests and take blame for the natural failures that will inevitably occur in any building without an owner.

He was a shammes. It was his job. It became his life.

He never tried to pretend he was important. A shammes is a glorified janitor, a good, solid, soldiering-forth job with a proper name in Yiddish, but the English translation, he knows, is *sexton*, which barely amounts to anything. A sexton is the helper candle on the menorah for Chanukah, the one that does not even require a blessing. He was a helper there, a guest. If they didn't need him to count in the quorum for prayer, who knew if they'd even pay him?

He never tried to pretend he was important. He knew he first received this position as a gesture of charity, a moment several years ago, back when he could have been full of possibility. He was soft-witted, perhaps, with a cloudy countenance, not as adroit as others, perhaps, but capable, at least at first glance, of many things—a business! a wife!—but instead he was entrusted with this synagogue.

And now, the ravages of—what? life? toil? just the act of staying on Earth, sticking around and not taking the easy way out?—had extracted its price on him, elongated his forehead into wrinkles, raisined his cheeks and eyes, and sandpapered his skin. He still didn't have much to show for his life, not if you ranked him against the other members of the minyan. No wife (though once, there was a woman), no children (although he gets along with them nearly always), no money to his name, not to speak of. But there was something else, something insubstantial but no less valuable, a marked change to the universe, a distinction between the *before you were here* and the *after you die* that would—he hoped, he prayed—somehow establish his own journey as a distinctive one.

The synagogue was a place that everyone passed through. No matter who you were, sooner or later you had to pray. But prayer was his livelihood. He arrived earlier than anyone else, and he was the last man to leave. If this were a battlefield, he'd be their secret weapon, their ace in the hole. In peacetime, he was caught in the thrall of the tide of early-morning responsibility, the voice of authority whose throbbing constant light shone as a beacon of moral superiority for the 6:45 morning minyan; he was the one who rose from his bed five minutes earlier than everyone else to have the synagogue unlocked, warmed up, the four Torahs arranged in their ark like a perfect family of doves, just to have it ready for the unappreciative masses; he was a mother.

His routine was a religion within itself. Every opening step, from the first scruff of his shoes on the welcome mat to scrubbing the doorpost mezuzah (inside were holy words, and the men kissed it when they walked past; it should be cleaned with disinfectant each day, the rabbi had instructed him, so people would not be afraid to keep kissing) to the draping of the synagogue tallises, the position of the crushed velvet curtain that hid the Torahs.

He was good at his job. He did not consider himself great at it—every action he took, mental or physical, Zaidy knew, was no great feat; he knew he expended the same amount of effort for simple thoughts that it took others to think of great, grand things—but if there were ever to be a Brotherhood of Meritorious Shammeses established, selected by some angel flying from synagogue to synagogue across the world, he would hope his services would, at least, be considered. He did his job thoroughly, and well, and he was trusted by the congregation to keep doing it. He was dependable and invisible; they expected no less. No more, but no less.

So it was with no small amount of irritation that he showed up one Monday morning shortly before sunrise—the clocks had been recently turned to daylight savings time, but nature had yet to catch up—to find Velvel Bieber perched on the stone front stairs, looking peckish and impatient and fiddling with the locked doors all on his own, as if he expected the handle to pop open of its own accord or in recognition of his seniority. His sloped face was even jowlier than usual. He had long sticklike arms and legs, and he moved as if he had just learned how, swallowed up by his black-brimmed hat and ill-fitting black suit. Velvel had lived in this area since he was a child—his grandparents were some of the first Jews to move to this neighborhood, and his parents were among the last to move away. Velvel Bieber tended to behave with other people's property as if it were his own, both respectful and egotistical, lifting up and fiddling with phones, computers, wallets even, with the utmost reverence and mindlessly investigating all of their inner depths. This morning, however, he was occupied entirely with the two handles of the two doors—left and right—which it was Zaidy's province, exclusively, to unlock.

He knew it was possible. The doorknobs and locks were last replaced eight years ago, cheap front-of-the-store tin things, and they were loose, untightened, liable to pop open, but not by Velvel Bieber's hand. Zaidy knew that if you gripped the left knob with your thumb at the very bottom of the flattened sphere, and all four fingers squeezed very tightly on the upper half, the knob would rattle in its socket. Yank hard enough, and it would pop.

But Velvel Bieber did not squeeze. Most people, Zaidy thought, had no idea—they came and went like the weather. Velvel didn't look grateful to him for showing up early. He didn't look much of anything at all. "Did you get cold waiting?" Zaidy offered, springing as much friendliness out of the question as he could possibly muster.

"Long enough," said Velvel, so low it was almost a thought. He brushed past Zaidy and through the doors. The synagogue was still a chamber of ice. Zaidy adjusted the thermostat manually. If he didn't get in so early, it wouldn't be worth doing. Prayers were thirty-five, forty minutes long, quicker if Wrinkle led, and by the time the synagogue warmed up, it was almost time to leave. They'd gotten these two space heaters in October, the kind that ran up the electric bill pretty high, and the rabbi didn't want to say anything, but Rosencranz, who knew about these things, said the electricity would be a strain on the synagogue's budget, and they were already stretching. Any time someone mentioned the budget, it killed whatever discussion they were having entirely.

Bais Matana was the synagogue. Literally the name meant the House of Matana, although it was, to be exact, a house without Matana. When construction went up in the '50s, Rabbi Walsh himself decided to name the building after Matana Goldman, the owner and president of Goldman's, the successful department store, and still very much involved in its day-to-day operations. Matana Goldman was a generous benefactor to the community. Because of him, children were sent to summer camp and their parents enjoyed evenings of blissful quietude, and poor families were provided with hot challah and sweet wine on their Shabbos tables every week. He donated gymnasiums, playgrounds, school buses. So what was a mere synagogue in the mix?

"It was the straw that broke the ass's back, that's what it was," Mr. Rosencranz told Zaidy one day. His eyes perpetually bulged out like an accusation, and his stiff white beard stuck out nearly horizontally, jabbing like an accusatory finger. "These filthy rich people who can't keep their money to themselves. They'll do basically anything. Only one thing you have to remember: You never tell them who's boss."

"I won't tell them who's boss," Zaidy replied, wise as ever.

Rabbi Walsh meant to tell Goldman about his namesake earlier. He picked out the date and time with care and caution, one Sunday morning after praying. However, he clammed up due to nerves, and Matana Goldman first heard of the plan by reading about it in the local Yiddish newspaper. So incensed was he by the assumption of his patronage that he authored an angry letter to the paper, vowing not to pay for one penny of the synagogue's construction, and to never set foot inside its doors—not even if it was the last synagogue in Brooklyn. This vow he maintained for nearly forty years, breaking it only when Bais Matana (in spite of his efforts, the name stuck) really *was* the only synagogue left—at which point he would enter one day a year, recite the prayer for mourners, and depart as soon as services ended, never saying a word.

During that day, Zaidy knew enough to stay clear of him. Certain things about the building's operation he left to those more skilled in such areas. The finances, the voting, anything to do with electricity. In other ways—among them, corralling this loose assortment into a collective single cohesive minyan—he was nothing short of an emperor.

Velvel Bieber withdrew to his pew near the center of the sanctuary and immersed himself in a book. Meanwhile, Zaidy performed his rituals. In his mind, every gesture worked to summon one of his congregants. Whether this was true, or whether this was a game he played with himself, was an unanswerable question. He had no clue whether straightening Rosencranz's chair actually caused the man to leave his house (and then to arrive here exactly four and a half minutes later), but he straightened it anyway; somewhere in G-d's infinitely complicated universe, there must be some conjoining link. After Rosencranz's chair, then the rabbi's. He readjusted the armrests, plumped the lopsided pancake pillows. The pews on the right, from back to front, and then the left ones. They squealed when he moved them, but that was the only way he could. With each squeak, Velvel Bieber gave a swift, caustic inhalation of breath through a bountiful forest of rustling nose hair.

"Do you have to?"

"Mr. Bieber, I have to. I can't lift it myself, each bench."

"Try to keep it down, then. I'm meditating."

"Oh, you're meditating." Zaidy knew he'd heard the word before but wasn't sure how. Repeating a word you didn't know back to the speaker, he'd found, was often a helpful way of mitigating his lack of knowledge.

"I'm getting my mind, y'know, accustomed. Getting it all ready to pray."

"I understand. I'll be quiet."

"Thank you."

Velvel Bieber went back to doing nothing. Zaidy let out a breath.

"Only one thing, Mr. Bieber—"

"Zaidy, I *told* you."

"I need to roll the Torah. Today is the new month. Can you help?"

"Zaidy, I just started with my tallis—"

Velvel Bieber's tallis had been sitting on his shoulder for five minutes. Usually he swept his fingers through its tassel, checking for broken fibers, then swifted it over his head and around his shoulders and chest, but today he wasn't doing much of anything.

"It's fine," Zaidy said. "I'll bring it out myself. The rabbi will do it when he comes."

"That's ridiculous." Velvel tossed aside his tallis to the pew and rose. "I'll help."

The congregation's Torahs were sealed in a fireproof safe. Zaidy dialed the combination lock with deliberate prudence, balancing the wheel between the fingers of both hands. He aimed each number on the combination wheel carefully against the arrow. The Torah they were using today was the heaviest one, thin and tall, its handles still displaying a glint of the new year's polish. He struggled to remove it alone. Velvel Bieber's arms reached past his, lifting out the Torah like a baby, depositing it in the cradle of Zaidy's grasp. He carried it to the podium. They wound the scroll back to the day's reading, Zaidy winding and Velvel catching, rolling the two wood columns like the axles of a car. The columns of calligraphed letters swirled by in fast motion, like watching a television show. Velvel's lips moved silently, measuring the verses until they reached the spot. Their eyes fluttered over the letters. Zaidy watched Velvel. He could see traces of a smile forming on Velvel's face, the grin of knowing he was needed, G-d needed you to be in this exact spot at this exact moment, there was no one else who could do this task except you—Zaidy recognized this feeling. He knew it well.

"Now stop," Velvel commanded, and Zaidy stopped winding. They wrapped the Torah back up, dressed it, and put it in the safe. A gravelly, high voice warbled a tune from the back of the sanctuary: the song that was sung during the prayer service while returning the Torah to its Ark. That, he knew without looking, would be Wrinkle Posen. Short, with tinted wraparound glasses (for his hypersensitive eyes, though Wrinkle insisted they made him look like a movie star) and multiple layers of sweatshirts, Wrinkle was always at synagogue early for no other reason than he had nowhere else to be. When middle-aged men turned into old men, their normal-people bodies either ballooned out or shriveled up, and Wrinkle was a prime example of the latter case. He'd never been big, but now he was a downright miniature version of his old self. He barked out a warm, hearty belch of a laugh—he was laughing at himself—and settled himself in the back row.

It was nearing their usual starting time now, and Rosencranz had also arrived. Wrinkle started reading Psalms, and Rosencranz was wrapping tefillin around his arm, which was crunched into an L-shape, exposing a well-developed muscle, the kind of muscle suitable for a man thirty or forty years Rosencranz's junior. The small black box sat atop his muscle like a dare.

Zaidy checked the time. 6:40. Four of them—no, six, since Getzel was coming through the door now, mopping his wet neck in a towel, and he'd probably gotten a ride from Dr. Gordon. They would definitely be seven; the rabbi would enter in five minutes exactly, as was his custom.

They still needed three more. Zaidy ran through his list of tasks for the morning, the daily machinations that kept the world in orbit. What had he forgotten? The seat pillows? The mezuzah?

He paced the room. Rosencranz had started praying now, and his buzz sent a charge of urgency through the room. The others were wrapping themselves in their ghostly tallises, binding themselves in the leather straps of their tefillin. Velvel Bieber drummed the pew in front of him with the fingers of one hand, impatient to launch into the call-and-response of kaddish already. Dr. Gordon's nose exploded radiantly into a tissue.

The tissue box! Zaidy felt the electric shock of a sudden remembering. Dr. Gordon was a surfer—that explained *that*—but Knaidel Krauss always had the sniffles, and the tissue box was the magic charm that would deliver him there. Zaidy ran to replace it, and as soon as he deposited the empty box in the rubbish bin, the old man waddled in.

"Mr. Krauss!" said Zaidy. "Your prayer book," offering up Knaidel's preferred sort of prayer book (Ashkenazic edition, Hebrew-only, blue cover). As he proffered it, Zaidy glanced at the clock. Five minutes! Right according to schedule, the door popped open again.

"Nu?" said a voice that cracked into the morning like a whip into flesh.

Zaidy could tell, without turning around, that the rabbi had arrived.

"Two to go," Rabbi Walsh said uselessly. Saying it didn't make them come. Of course they were two men short. Zaidy was the shepherd.

Zaidy went to the phone. The synagogue kept an old rotary phone in the rear, tucked away in a peeling cabinet behind the Purim decorations—for emergencies, the rabbi reminded them constantly. Out came the list of telephone numbers, almost as old as the synagogue itself. Most of them had been crossed out.

"Try Gavin," Wrinkle said. "Give him a break from the kids."

Zaidy's thumb ran down the handwritten scrawls of names. Rubin, Cohen, Broflovski—all had moved away. A dozen other names, all scratched out, some violently enough to be rendered illegible, some determinedly enough to wear holes in the paper. You find a new house, a better house, in a nicer part of the city, or somewhere away from the city, somewhere more appropriate to raise your family. *This neighborhood is changing,* Rosner, the plumber, told him one day. *You're lucky. You're big enough so they don't mess with you.* That was shortly before he packed up his seven kids—the ones still living at home—and moved to Monsey.

Rosner had been one of his favorites. His children, so polite and restrained when they came to him for their Saturday morning lollipop. Zaidy wished one day he could return the favor.

"Gavin won't be able to," said Knaidel. "His wife's got the flu, and he has to take care of the kids. She was up half the night, hacking away."

Knaidel lived in the same building as Gavin and his family, in the apartment directly below them. Wrinkle gave a birdlike scowl. "You were listening for half the night, is that right, Knaidel?" he said. "What were you listening *for?*"

Wrinkle could say things like that, things no one else could. He noticed things that nobody else did too. Zaidy had to be careful of him. Of all the weekday morning regulars, Wrinkle would probably be the first to notice Zaidy's secret.

"Aw, shove it! It ain't like that." Knaidel threw up his hands. "Zaidy, why don't you give a call to Brubaker? He hasn't been here in weeks."

"Brubaker moved away last month," said Wrinkle. "That's why you haven't seen him."

"Less and less of us left," murmured Rosencranz.

"We'll get someone," Zaidy said firmly.

He dialed Brubaker's number anyway. He knew it had been disconnected, but it bought him time, his somber dialing, listening to that soft and certain voice in his ear, informing him. Then he called Gavin. As he expected, it went straight to voicemail.

They were getting itchy. The clock was churning ever forward; time was on nobody's side. It was close to seven now, and still no minyan.

"Do you want me to help with that, Zaidy?" The rabbi pressed close, too close. He might catch a glimpse of the paper with the phone list. Zaidy snatched it up, pressed it into his chest, face down. "Relax," the rabbi continued, uninterrupted, a constant drone, no surprises in anything he said, ever. "We're only trying to help."

"I'll try one more number," Zaidy said, his voice modulated, his soul screaming for help from above. Attendance was lackadaisical, people had been running late all month, but it was never as bad as this.

"But we need two more men," said Rosencranz humorlessly.

The door slammed open, then slammed shut. A flurry of outside air snatched all their attention. "How many more are we?" said Matt breathlessly, hands against the door, slithering out of his incredibly long scarf. Matt, who'd just moved into their neighborhood with his wife, both of them equally young. Childless. Nobody was sure what they were doing here. They postdated everyone by decades. Their motives in wanting to live here were uncertain, unfathomable.

"We're nine," barked Rosencranz, a little too eager to pull the trigger. "We need one more man to start prayers."

"Did anyone call Gavin?" Matt said. His scarf was still coming off—this was ridiculous, several yards long, completely impractical. Matt was a young man trying to look like an old man, but the clothes he wore were clothes that no old man had ever worn in Manhattan Beach. Several-hundred-dollar retro spectacles, jackets that clung to his body in such a way as Wrinkle or Knaidel would never permit. Zaidy was breathing heavier now, sweating a cold and nervous sweat. They were on to him. Rosencranz, at least. He had to know.

"Gavin's wife is sick," said Knaidel, then chuckled. "No fun for him last night."

Matt pulled away from him, as if Knaidel's distastefulness were contagious.

"Then who's left?" asked Matt.

"Bieber, Getzel, Rosencranz," the rabbi ran through his inventory, listing names that should have already been plain to him, the people who were already watching him. "Knaidel, Dr. Gordon, and Mr. Posen." He ticked off his fingers. "And me . . . and you, Zaidy . . . and this young man . . ." He didn't know Matt's name; he was too new, or too strange, to stick long in Rabbi Walsh's memory.

"That's it," said Velvel Bieber. "You're going to have to get Goldman."

"Now, hold on," the rabbi said. "Let's be reasonable."

Dr. Gordon gave one of those loud *tkk*s that was supposed to be in his head, but so the rest of them could hear. "I'm sorry, Rabbi, I have to get to work."

"It doesn't have to be Goldman," said the rabbi. "Someone else might be coming—"

"Who else?" said Dr. Gordon. "Who else is there?"

The minyan fell silent. It seemed that the room itself was breathing now: the measured labor of the heating system, a grinding, prolonged, ill, and whiny wheeze. Zaidy's skin burned ferociously, not from the radiators but from the weight of the secret about to implode.

"There's no one," said the rabbi, his voice the voice of the synagogue itself, of all those bottled-up years of construction and crumbling, a deep and rumbling thing, so that when he spoke it was the voice of authority, of prophecy, it was G-d's own voice. Even when he spoke a question, or an opinion, there was a single caustic moment when he fell silent where no one dared disagree, both because of his words and the air around them, a realization that hit them all at once, a wave to bowl them all over equally. There were strangers who made their way to the synagogue, certainly—Shabbos guests, visitors, family, the old Russians who traveled from a mile down the boardwalk to stand mutely as the others prayed and then to receive a bowl of Wrinkle's saucy cholent after services, but no one else lived here any longer, no one else ever came; nobody could remember the last time a soul had shown up, a soul who was not one of them. The men inside these walls—them, and Gavin, and no one else—were the surviving minyan of Bais Matana.

"So, it's Gavin or Goldman," mused Velvel Bieber. "No one else."

"Not Goldman," said Dr. Gordon. "He's never wanted to be a part of this place. He's always wished us ill."

"But a mitzvah is a mitzvah," said Getzel in a singsong.

"He's come here before," Zaidy added, trying to be helpful. "To say kaddish for his wife."

They all looked to the rabbi for an answer.

"We can't force Gavin," he said. "His wife is incapacitated, and he has children. A kindness is a kindness."

"So, it's Goldman, then," said Zaidy softly, disbelieving the moment.

No one was willing to speak. Finally, it was Rosencranz who stoked the fire, who set it all in motion. He turned to Zaidy, laid a warm and gnarled paw on his shoulder.

"Go get Goldman," he said.

Zaidy layered on his coat and hat and scarf. It was early March, barely winter in most parts of the city, but here the winds burned with a fury that was collected out over the cold, cruel openness of ocean, summoning up force and fury as they traveled inland. In the places where the blocks broke, there were no buildings to stop the torrent, and the winds slammed pedestrians at every street crossing with all the full force of winter's last call.

It was payback, he told himself. Payback for letting Velvel Bieber wait in the cold.

He once thought he could have a wife. At one point it was a possibility, and then more than a possibility: "You have what everyone else has," said Cousin Yossel, the rabbi, the patriarch of his brownstone family, shaking him so hard he heard his skin slap against his bones. "What more could a girl want?"

He was dispatched to a matchmaker, a woman in her fifties, not unattractive herself, seated at a desk and flanked by stacks of sheets. A wisp of her dark exotic wig fell tantalizingly over one eye.

"Siddown!" she growled. One word, one syllable. Without even thinking of doing otherwise, he sat.

Over the course of hours, she quizzed him on his entire life—what he did at the synagogue, what jobs he'd done before that, his relationship with the people he worked with, his life growing up in the sanatorium, how old was he when his parents passed and how he felt about it. He did not normally think of such things—in fact, it had been several years since he'd seriously thought of the accident—but he did not collapse into tears. He did not smash his head against the desk until it bled. He answered with the same slow, precise, wise tongue with which he always spoke. He was a prophet. He was a sage.

After that, all she had was one last question. "But what do you *want?*" she asked him. "From a wife? From your life?"

Zaidy abandoned the taut, restrained, complacent tone with which he addressed everything. This was one answer he didn't even have to pretend to think about. He'd known it his whole life.

"Kids," he said. "I want to have kids."

As soon as he left the matchmaker's office, the despair hit. There was no way. There was no one. He didn't even have friends outside the synagogue; he could never keep someone's attention through a conversation, let alone through meeting and dating and 120 years of marriage. But then he asked himself, how much worse off was he than before he'd gone to meet the matchmaker? He wasn't, not at all. So, it was one thing to cross off his list. He'd officially tried to get married. Now he could remain in his cozy solitary nook of an apartment forever.

That was when he really started to embrace the kids—not potential children inside his mind but the ones who already did exist. At Bais Matana, there were still dozens, back then, whole underage armies of them, swarming the pews. He stopped yelling heated retorts in response to the recurring taunts of the older ones. When the younger ones asked why he looked so big, was he an ogre, why wasn't his face the same on both sides—instead of losing it, he started to flash a goofy smile, as though they were telling a joke. If he couldn't make his own children, then at least he could be like a father to the rest of them. For Sabbath he bought a monstrous bag of candy, carried it to synagogue, lavished its contents on the children who came to him. Had it been anybody else, people might have regarded it as a slap in the face to Dr. Gordon, the existing candy man, a successful dentist who doled out a measly single Tootsie Roll per child. But Dr. Gordon crumpled up his bag and beamed. "He deserves it," Dr. Gordon told the other men at kiddush, over matjes herring and a thimble of scotch. "He's like the zaidy they never had."

She called back. She gave him a name—a single name. "Her name is Neshama," said the matchmaker. "Can you remember that? Can you say it to me?"

"Neshama," he said.

"Keep on saying it. That was okay, but lumpy. You need to practice. A girl wants to hear her name roll off your tongue like a song. Repeat it to yourself every day, at home, over and over. You live alone, don't you?"

"I live alone," said Zaidy.

"Good. No girlfriends ever come over, do they? You got a nurse or something, any caregivers?"

"My cousins," he said. "I have them once a week for tea. I bring them cakes from the shop. I get juice for the kids."

"Good, good. Now this girl you're seeing, this Neshama. She has a lady who comes with her, who takes care of her sometimes. If anything happens, G-d willing, she'll come to visit you two every day; you won't have to take special care of her, you just let the other lady do it. Do you understand?"

"I understand," he said.

"Neshama is very important. You're not an easy person to set up, you understand. And Neshama Goldman, she is a catch. A one in a million. You won't get another chance like this."

"That's why I'm here," said Zaidy.

They met at her father's house. The matchmaker had instructed him to come on time—not early and not late—and not to gawk or appear surprised. She said this knowing it would not work, but she said it anyway. When Zaidy showed up, his jaw hung slack, flapping up and down with the pace of his slowing legs and the rustle of the beach breeze. Neshama's house bordered the water, the last house before the sand began. Twin rows of Roman columns led him up the stairs. A pagoda porch's roof was set just high enough to avoid the neighbors' second-story windows, rimmed by the open night, so its inhabitants, whoever they were—the building was big enough to hold hundreds—could drink or dine at leisure, away from scrying eyes. Beyond it was a row of hatched prismatic doors. Beyond that was Neshama.

She had thick black hair to keep her warm from the wind tunnels, and the whites of her eyes were big as silver dollars. She introduced herself solely by speaking her name, once, although that was the lone thing about her that Zaidy already knew. Her hands clutched the protective rails as she guided herself to the table. He pulled the seat back, as a gentleman should, and let her sit down before seating himself.

She listened to Zaidy with an intensity he'd never before received. They sat on that porch for hours into the night, and the fire in the hearth must have burned through half a tree—her nurse appeared to stoke it; in her speckless white frock and hat, she would unlock the twin protective gates that kept them from tending to the fire themselves. She changed the records on the phonograph, massaging their conversation with a light, airy jazz—not the new jazz that was coming out of Harlem but a jaunty, easy jelly-roll jazz that kept them feeling happy and innocent. And when the matchmaker called the next day, asking how it had gone, Zaidy had no choice but to confess the truth: he was, he thought, in love.

Her tone was positive but practical. "So, you'd like to proceed, then?" she said. "You aren't bothered by her disability?"

Oh, he knew what she was talking about, he wasn't immune to noticing these things: the limp she walked with, the void between her eyebrows and her hairline; her delay in finishing sentences, which was more pronounced than his own—Neshama hadn't been practicing for years to cover it up like Zaidy had; most times when she spoke, she forgot the end before she reached it. But those things weren't what was important to him. She was important to him.

"Oh, no," he said. "Oh, yes."

"Very well, then. I'll telephone Neshama's father and say we'd like the go-ahead to proceed."

He took her on walks, along the boardwalk and through the checkerboard streets. He showed her his favorite places, the stores where he shopped and his favorite windows: the pet shop, the watchmaker, the mannequin store. They went to the magic shop and tried the wood and the plastic puzzles. She took whole minutes deliberating each turn, but she was surprisingly good at solving them.

Neshama walked with a slowness that could be suffocating—she was very well cared for; except with him, she rarely left the house—but he had patience and kept pace with her and always turned back as soon as she tired. He showed her every kindness; he, after all, had once been in her very same position. He used his salary from the bake shop to buy her cakes and hot dogs and small stuffed animals. Once, he bought her a porcelain doll that looked just like her—dark velvety hair, pale skin untouched by the sun, huge and perfectly round marble eyes that never closed. She clutched it to her chest and carried it with her whenever they met, an omnipresent extra party to their peregrinations.

They walked down the boardwalk, and held hands before marriage; even though it was not their custom, people from the community smiled at them, bestowing upon them an implicit permission. It was more than just permission. It was their blessing. She spoke to him in her father's native Hungarian, luminous, flowing, threaded syllables that to him had no meaning but soon became his favorite sound in the world. He took her to Coney Island on the bus. Together there they marveled at the freak show, gazed in mutual adoration at the sword-swallowers and contortionists and tattooed ladies, happy to finally be normal.

The nurse trailed behind them like a shadow, always lunging forward when Neshama would trip or stumble, but she was affable and as charmed by them as the rest of the world. When they bade her to, she would go off to purchase them sodas or to telephone home and ask what was for dinner or to fall asleep, hat sloping down her tied-taut hair, her button nose lodged between the pages of a ladies' magazine, as Zaidy and Neshama whispered to each other secrets.

The first time they made love, in his apartment, they finally stumbled upon something they shared an equal ineptness at. They fumbled; they taught each other how each other's respective clothes came off, the mystery of what unfastened where, how different garments broke apart. He showed her how he preserved his ties, hanging, too complicated to retie but easily loosened and tightened around his neck. They laughed at each other. They laughed at themselves. They stared at each other's bodies in the dusky curtain-filtered light. They made each other feel extraordinary; each was accustomed to asking for what they needed, frank and unabashed, and each cared about nothing so much as doing exactly what the other requested.

Matana Goldman himself was the biggest supporter of their union. She was his only daughter; after his wife died, his only family; his empire was singularly devoted to making her happy. He almost always greeted Zaidy at the door himself, always with a smile and a piece of advice. Other than for Zaidy, he would never answer the door on his own. He was a private man, with little desire to communicate with other members of the human race; just seeing Zaidy come to the door, carrying his box of bakery cookies and brightening his daughter, made Matana Goldman come alive. And watching them depart together, off on another of their promenade walks, made him miss his own departed wife so profoundly that he could cry from a perfect happiness.

She called him late at night, after she was sure her father was asleep. "I miss you," he said. Those words, through the dull mouthpiece of the phone. He heard his own echo. It sounded insufficient.

"I miss you too," she told him. "I think I'm going to have a baby."

"How do you know?"

She struggled. Her limited vocabulary, the boundaries of modest talk. She could think of nothing appropriate to say.

"I can tell it," she said. "I know I'm going to be a mommy."

"I am so happy."

He was so happy. He could think of no more significant way to tell her—"I love you," he said.

"I love you too," she told him.

They hung up. Each of them in their respective bedroom, elated. They couldn't wait to see each other again.

He didn't know what'd happened to her. Not at first. At first everything was going so well. Love letters, messages, gifts from her father on his doorstep—new shirts, a leatherbound book of Psalms, a case of cigars. And then it wasn't.

It happened one night. For the first hours, he was unaware anything was wrong. The first notice came from the matchmaker, in the morning.

"I'm sorry," she said. "This isn't going to be a wedding."

He remembered being called to Neshama's house. It was the first time he'd been inside for more than a few minutes. A pair of cousins accompanied him. They hung back by the door, looking harried and out of place and ready to run away. Zaidy, alone, approached Mr. Goldman on the couch. His bulbous shining head—thin hedges of hair on both sides like a crown—hung between his legs. He had sitting to each side an attendant, business partners maybe, two men in nearly identical suits. They were supposed to be comforting him, but they both looked out of place, uncomfortable, like they wanted to be invisible and couldn't get it right. They stared at Zaidy like an unwelcome intruder.

When Mr. Goldman saw Zaidy, he got up. His eyes were red and tiny. They pulled back far into that gargantuan turtle head of his. He hugged Zaidy. No one else had ever gotten that close to him, hugged him so fully of their own volition, had let that much of their body touch Zaidy's. He felt like it was Neshama.

He didn't see Mr. Goldman much after that. On the street, at the kosher supermarket. He never said anything to him. The last time they spoke was at the funeral, when Zaidy waited in the receiving line with the other well-wishers, shuffling forward at intervals to bid his respects. Mr. Goldman rose when he saw him. He leaned across the table, and Zaidy wondered if they were going to hug again. Instead, Mr. Goldman leaned tight into his ear and spoke through gritted teeth. "She was always so close to being broken," he said. "What made you think she could withstand a *baby?*" He snarled the last word like a curse. That was the end.

He released Zaidy, and Zaidy had the distinct impression that he was being dismissed. It didn't much matter—the gravesite part of the service was occurring in Montefiore Cemetery, in Queens, and Zaidy had neither car nor driver. Outside on the boulevard, the sun cruelly bright in his eyes and the sky like a beach, he told himself it was probably for the best. It was winter, the sun would be fading soon, and he had to prepare the synagogue for the sunset prayer.

Sometimes he thought of the synagogue as his own child. It constantly required his attention, needed cleanings and changings, never did what you wanted it to. The old men whined constantly, until he made everything right with the world, and then, a new miracle every time, they quieted up like falling asleep.

It was years ago that he'd last stood in this pagoda. He hadn't been young then; neither of them had—cases such as theirs took more time than other couples to find the perfect match—but he was much older now. How many times had they sat there, watched the fire being stoked, talking in whispers about a future neither of them could fully fathom? He rang the bell. He knew quite well no one would come to the door. Mr. Goldman never answered the door himself, and the housekeeper wouldn't be in this early. Early for the rest of the world, but late for them: the minyan was impatient for him; the rabbi was probably twitching; Mr. Goldman better agree to come right away.

He felt a clock ticking in his head. With every click, a new anxiety.

Except that Mr. Goldman wouldn't be asleep. He had the same commitments as the rest of them. Goldman's own synagogue, the one that he supported, the other synagogue in town—Congregation Ahavas Chumras was its name—had long ago stopped holding its daily prayers and finally shut its doors for good last year; Zaidy had heard talk that the building was in negotiations to be purchased by an Indian church. But Mr. Goldman still had to pray. He was probably awake right now, already wrapped in his own tallis and tefillin, possibly engaged in one of the parts of prayer that you couldn't interrupt with speech.

"Mr. Goldman?" Zaidy rang the chime. He heard its dim echo through the front door. He touched the handle. Then he squeezed and turned.

The door swung open. Its hinges were well-oiled; neither the synagogue doors nor the door to his apartment opened with that cushy-feeling automaticness. The carpet was thick. Each step felt both luxurious and intrusive. A part of his brain was warning Zaidy not to be here, to run back to the synagogue, to retreat with his excuse: he called out and no one responded. Another part of his brain was telling him he had every right to be here. In another time, another reality, he might have been here instead of the synagogue.

He passed through the vestibule, the drawing room, the kitchen. There were several rooms that looked like living rooms or lounge rooms, more than anyone could ever conceivably lounge in. On a side table in a narrow hallway sat a prayer book. Zaidy noted the page it was open to, right at the very beginning. The blessings that thanked G-d for opening your eyes, for giving you sight and speech and everything you needed. Then he realized the chair next to the prayer book was occupied. The man was draped in a tallis, wrapped so completely you could barely notice his head.

"Mr. Goldman!" Zaidy was astounded. Relief swept through him, relief and surprise and reward. Entering the house hadn't been a vain effort at all; his actions had purpose, and motive, and he had succeeded in his goal. It wasn't until all these feelings had zigzagged through him like charges of static electricity, discharging painlessly into the floor, that Zaidy felt as though perhaps he had not followed the most prudent course of action. Thoughts of trespassing—and interrupting, and invading—sprang into his head. Zaidy bent down to address him face to face. He looked into those unforgiving eyes.

He might have stood there ten seconds or an hour. He didn't fully understand until he touched the man's wrist and felt the deep cold.

In Jewish law it is forbidden to leave a corpse alone. A shomer, or watchman, is necessary to stand over the body from the moment of death until burial: to protect it, to guard whatever bits of soul are left inside, and to fend off whatever loneliness might hit before it is consecrated into the packed embrace of earth.

Zaidy didn't always remember these laws, the ones you didn't follow every day, but right now he remembered this one. After venturing briefly into the next rooms in both directions, finding a nearby phone and calling the synagogue, Zaidy returned to that narrow hallway side table at which Matana Goldman's stiffened body sat. He pulled around the other chair so that they faced each other, and he settled in for what could be a while. He had so much to tell Mr. Goldman, now that he had a moment; so many answers to the questions that they had probably both wrestled with, answers that he thought Mr. Goldman might want to hear.

But before he could share them, there was something he had to do. Zaidy shut the prayer book and carried it back to the bookshelf. He located the vacancy at once. Tenderly, not disturbing the books on either side of the gap, he slid the prayer book in, corner first, then straightening it, releasing the spine only once it stood shoulder to shoulder with the books to its left and right. That was what he was good at. That was what he did.

Originally published in The Cincinnati Review

Merryn Rutledge

Mary Magdalene on Sunday

I went to see what was left of him—
not in the tomb, in me.
Bright morning sun making me blink,
my tearing eyes to blur.
All around, the ground lay steeped in sorrow
after a two-days' rain.

Along the way, no one.
I stumbled on, weary from lack of sleep,
as in a labor that aches,
then cracks you open hour upon hour,
slowly, slowly.
You cannot know what the birth will bring.

Last week was labor, too, only then
I knew where we were heading,
he and I. Even so,
how dread dragged across the days.
Because Jesus was the kind of man
who, having started, must go to the end.

But this grief is the hardest work of all.
I stopped to rest
where there could be none—
at the mouth of the forbidding cave.
I would wait
for what silence might send.

He came
quietly, like when we knelt to pray
at home, or on the road, at the end of the day.
All those years, together approaching
the great, empty temple
where pure presence dwells.

I don't know how else but this to explain—
an opening in the womb of sorrow
through which I sensed emerging—
the two of us going on and on.
I, carrying him as past and as present
I can bear.

Heidi Seaborn

Even Now, After all These Years

Each shift in motion begins with one bird's fear, a feather trigger.
Maybe it's a wind uptick or the startle of reflection in the Wadden Sea

that sets the starlings' murmuration. Millions, black in flight, in dance,
in Denmark. A form of madness, the starlings chattering in a single voice.

For love of Shakespeare, we speak starling, our mouths black with feathers.
I want to dance. But you refuse to lead. Isn't that a form of backstepping,

of creating space between us? One could say it is sacred, the wingspan
of distance from your body to mine. We could hold a lit candle or a child

within the chapel of light between us. The European starlings arrived
in crates as a gift of improvement to the New World—

a sonnet of birdsong released into Central Park. Word travels with speed.
So, when you tell me you still love me, it flies past me.

Say it again, louder so my heart can hear. You know I'm a flight risk.

Once, we found each other before a congregation, vowing unison. Last night, your body folded around mine, holding

my fears in the nest of your hands. We slept like that as starlings swept the night sky before rising into their Black Sun.

Stunning you say, meaning the murmuration of birds, meaning me— improbable beauty on an otherwise ordinary day.

Originally published in The Missouri Review

Julie Marie Wade

The Plague of Locusts

You have lived long enough to know that every love story sounds apocryphal, especially when it's true. The fact that Angie saw you in a crowded room, her gaze alighting, then flitting away, then returning with every intention not to linger—but lingering anyway—sounds apocryphal. The fact that you saw her, too, wrapped in a long pistachio sweater you now keep in a cedar chest, her cornflower eyes flashing heedful and keen, and thought *green! blue! world!* with such furious delight that you instantly foretold she would become so—your world, that is—sounds apocryphal. And the fact that this was only the first day of a ten-day orientation, summarily referred to as The Orientation—words printed in blocky chalk at the top of the board and in an officious font on the header of your handouts—sounds apocryphal enough to border on the absurd. Yet who could deny the way you oriented toward each other, leaning in almost to the point of tipping, desperate not to miss anything the other said or did, and in a manner destined to result in imbrication? That was in fact a word you both learned *at* The Orientation. The director said, "Think of the way tiles on certain roofs overlap to create a textured pattern. That's imbricated roofing. Or think of the way layers of tissue overlap as they grow in and gradually seal a wound. That's imbricated healing. We want our students to read and write that way, attending to the places of overlap between texts, between ideas. Fewer divisions and more connections. That's imbricated learning in a nutshell." It was also another way of naming love. Once upon a time, you were a gawky preteen so afraid of the phenomenon yet so infatuated with it—love, that is—that you let a boy lift you onto his shoulders at a church retreat—you, in your dripping suit with your gooseflesh legs—to fight a girl you barely knew. She too was raised like a soggy flag onto another boy's anonymous shoulders and without any coaxing at all began to kick and swipe. A stuffy room reeking of chlorine, the conspicuous absence of all chaperones, a crowd of classmates whooping from bleachers and pool: "Knock her down! Knock her down!" For this was the lore: the girl who fell would end up unrequited, while the girl who caused her fall would never want for love. The boys beneath wielded your bodies like lances, thrusting you toward each other. There was a moment when your face came so close to the other girl's—her freckles particular then as grains of sand, the golden hairs that rimmed her temples drying faster than her long, brown braid—and in that moment, you glimpsed a future where such collisions might be tender, purposeful, and frequent. You felt her warm breath pass over your cheek and almost smiled—how could you help yourself?—just before she coiled her fist and released it hard against your mouth. The onlookers deemed this a "sucker punch," worthy of loud applause. You tumbled backwards with a huge splash, not far from the ledge and lucky to have cleared it. Even underwater, you could hear their cheers, the chanting of the other girl's name: "Nancy! Nancy!" You could feel your lips already swelling, the burn of that inverted kiss, your first, that would soon deepen and purple with shame. Later the pastor, exasperated, would ask: "Just how many popsicles have you had?" When you answered "None," you knew he didn't believe you. Perhaps no one ever had. Now it's present-day, and Angie calls in a panic: "You won't believe this, Julie! It's happening, and I don't even really believe it, but—I think I'm caught in a swarm of locusts. Is that possible?" You stand at the window in the home you share: bright sun and smooth blue stretching horizonward, a few wisps of soft white fringe. "What do you mean?" She is driving through central Florida and, to hear her explain, the sky went dark at midday like something biblical. (You were both brought up this way.) She thought it was thunder at first, or some kind of distant stampede; then, suddenly, the whole car was swallowed up in a cloud of them, the raucous—did she say *music?*—of insect bodies crashing against the glass and ricocheting away, back, away, back. The wipers couldn't keep up. Words like *frenzy*. Words like *chaos*. "Where are you now?" Pulled over on the shoulder, a line of cars with flashers on, and no one fool or brave enough to step outside. "Stay put!" your command, so obvious, but love hates more than anything to feel useless. At the computer now, you search for clues, finding that others before you have left a digital trail: *Are there locusts in Florida? Apocalyptic flying pests of the Southeast? Spring road hazards near Gainesville?* "Oh my God. They're *love bugs!*" you exclaim. "I always thought those were just a metaphor." She's besieged. She's braced and stationary behind the wheel. Over Bluetooth, you can hear them clattering like dishes in a cabinet, reminiscent of the earthquakes of your youth. "Love bugs?" she asks, incredulous. You click and click some more: "It says here that it's their mating season." You scroll and scroll some more: "Also called the double-headed bug or the honeymoon fly—many people confuse them with locusts because of the density of their swarms. During and after mating, conjoined pairs remain together, even in flight, for several days." Sometimes, love makes a spectacle of itself. Always, love is a risk. After twenty years together, joined even when apart, you have learned that love is often heightened patience, waiting together for something to come, for something else to pass. You stay on the line, imbricated as ever. "Did you know that some people believe love bugs are a hoax?" Angie scoffs. "Not anybody on this highway." You keep reading: "There's a conspiracy theory that love bugs aren't a natural phenomenon at all and don't actually exist in the wild." You can't see her, but you know she is shaking her lovely head, rolling her lovely eyes. "Well, this is pretty wild." One story goes that researchers at the University of Florida created love bugs in a lab, and then they got loose and began reproducing rapidly—a science experiment gone wrong. By now, you're both laughing, though it could be true. What couldn't? By now, the cataclysm (for years, you thought it was *catechism*) seems to be tapering off. Just a low hum in the background, a soft vibration like an aftershock. "It says here you can use dryer sheets to scrape away some of the guts, but most cleaning products aren't strong enough to do much good. Love bugs are particularly sticky." She makes her cautious way back to you near the bottom of the state. She follows the light and the sound of your voice, her GPS cutting in every now and then to reiterate its favorite mandate: "Proceed to the route." The next morning, you'll drive the car you share to the local wash. Sheepish as you roll down the window, you'll say, "Something happened on the way—" but the attendant interrupts with a summons you don't expect, bellowing: "LOVE BUGS!" Several men wielding push brooms appear from where? You never see them coming. They dip the bristles in buckets of green-blue fluid and begin their synchronous scrub. The car shakes with you inside it like a flight simulation. Sudden turbulence, then calm. Sudden turbulence, then calm. This too is a metaphor—for life, that is. You have never wanted to make of your love a spectacle, and yet, so often, you and your beloved pass through the world unnoticed, or mistaken for what you are not: roommates, friends, sisters even, and once, absurdly, twins. A certain mythos still surrounds the mathematics of you: two women, one bed, no men. To some, inconceivable. (Insert, if you must, a pun.) But now that secrets are no longer synonymous with love, you refuse the shrouds perpetually draped across your story— endless, they seem, as a magician's handkerchief. For the rest of your life, you will always be lifting a veil, always raising the coverlets designed to conceal. "Ma'am, please pull forward." You'll pull forward. "Looks like you had quite an encounter out there." You'll nod your head. "We do the best we can to remove this kind of residue, but love bugs tend to leave traces." It sounds apocryphal, so of course you know it's true.

Originally published in Ecotone

Will Wellman

To a Great Egret

There will be egrets in a few thousand years
who will have evolved without plumes so we cannot take them.
—Thylias Moss, "There Will Be Animals"

Masters Bayou is a body of water in St. Petersburg, Florida just past
the Gandy Bridge if coming west from Tampa. It sits south of Gandy
Boulevard, north of Weedon Island, and is closed in on all sides except
the east where it opens to Tampa Bay.

If you follow the northern coast of Masters Bayou west you'll first
pass a restaurant with a large, palm-thatched Tiki bar, where someone
standing in the sand will most likely be singing Tom Petty to the bar's
clientele; then a yacht company; a failed development, empty and
overgrown with trees and weeds, and the last home to coyotes and foxes
in the area; townhomes; a shipyard, which houses a giant ship, always
there, named Murphy's Law; some more townhomes; then, lastly, two
homes with expansive St. Augustine grass lawns. The coast to the south
is all mangroves, those beautiful marine trees with roots like thick, khaki
spiderweb spreading across the water.

At the very last moment, yards before the water ends, if you cut to
the left—the south—you will discover a tunnel entering the mangroves.
It's grown over and you probably think you can't make it, but you can.
Follow the water down the mangrove tunnel.

Chances are, once you get a few yards back, you'll find me. I'm in
a blue, sixteen-foot Mad River canoe with my friend Vince Chillura.
My parents have just moved to Weedon Island, and Vince and I are
exploring in this canoe I bought more than a decade ago in college.

And depending on when exactly you catch us, you might see a great egret flying just ahead through the tunnel, effortlessly gliding beneath the enclosing mangrove limbs.

*

Great egrets (*Ardea alba*) are large wading birds found on all continents except Antarctica. Unlike most egrets, they are placed in the heron genus *Ardea* and not *Egretta* wherein the smaller egrets reside. Great egrets stand over three feet tall with a long, snake-like neck and brilliant, white plumage on wings that can extend nearly six feet in width. In flight, the egret's long s-shaped neck compresses inwards until its head merges with the body, the neck looking like a giant Adam's apple.

I have seen great egrets throughout my life. However, it wasn't until I interned with the Audubon Society at Corkscrew Swamp Sanctuary that I came to truly appreciate them. Corkscrew Swamp—13,450 acres in the Western Everglades outside of Naples, Florida—was formed in the 1950s to protect one of the oldest bald cypress (*Taxodium distichum*) stands in North America, as well as to provide habitat for numerous rookeries. The sanctuary is considered the crown jewel of Audubon's sanctuary networks and a popular destination for birding due to its 2.25-mile boardwalk which winds through pine flats, wet prairie, marsh, and swamp.

My six-month internship provided an education in slowing down. Phone service was shoddy, and the shared computer in the office had the slowest dial-up internet I've ever encountered. To talk with family, I walked a quarter mile down the road until I got a bar or two of service. The intern's cabin, affectionately known as the Gator Hole, had no TV and a barely functioning AC unit. I had become separated from the many comforts and distractions of regular life.

I spent my free time exploring the swamp and other ecosystems in the sanctuary. I quickly came to learn the wading birds by name and recognize their peculiar habits. Some days I went deep into the sanctuary to watch dozens and dozens of gators sunbathe along old agricultural irrigation canals. I would often walk the whole day with no direction or purpose—errantly as Jim Corbett would put it.

I remember, especially, watching great egrets feed. There are a few swamp ponds along the boardwalk where you can always count on seeing wading birds. Great egrets stand on long, black-scaled legs over water still as statues. This sophistry tricks fish beneath the surface into thinking the birds are no danger, just a tree, limb, or some other inanimate object. And then suddenly, like a strike of lightning, the long white neck wakes to life driving toward water, the bird's school bus yellow bill spearing dinner.

The numerous tourists and birders would *ooh* and *ahh. Did you see how fast that bird was? Oh my gosh, that was crazy!* I understood their wonder at the egret's speed—the brevity of the meal—but I was struck more by the stillness. Something about the deliberateness of the bird, static over dark, tannin-stained waters, awoke in me a notion of some forgotten world, some deep wood far beyond.

*

One spring in college, before finals, I drove to Panama City for a weekend of revelry. Bored of the interstate, I pulled off down a state road lined with live oaks in Florida's Panhandle. Outside of Tallahassee I passed an alligator farm and on impulse pulled over. When I approached the farm, I found a locked chain-link fence.

Just as I turned back to my car, I heard a hushed southern voice ask, *Can I help you?* A forty-something man in wind-flapped overalls appeared—the owner of the gator farm. I mumbled something about being interested in the farm and wanting to look around. He graciously let me in.

Like numerous eccentric folks throughout the South, he was this brilliant, backwoods philosopher sort who decided on a whim to open a gator farm. A kind and quiet man, he walked me through the farm, telling me about the operation and the numerous gators that lived there. One bull gator had been penned up in solitary confinement, a punishment for his cannibalistic palate: he'd killed and eaten parts of two other bull gators.

As we walked through the farm, my guide wowed me with numerous facts about gators. American alligators (*Alligator mississippiensis*) have four-chambered hearts, unlike most three-chambered reptiles. During a dive, gators slow their heart rate down to two to three heartbeats a minute to conserve oxygen. And in the winter, gators will nestle up in a den and brumate—a reptilian version of hibernation—until temperatures rise above 55 ° F. He also mentioned, *they can go weeks, hell months, without me needing to feed them.*

We finally came to an open-air building with the constant sound of running water. Inside at a row of tanks, the man reached down, his hand disappearing to the elbow in water. It emerged with something small, greenish-black. Our eyes met, and he handed me the small thing: a baby gator, a foot long at most. That little gator writhing in my hand shocked me. The muted warmth of its body, the blood that coursed its veins—blood that has traversed this world for millennia—pumped in my hands. Panama City couldn't have been farther away.

*

A striking fact—birds are closer in relation to alligators than lizards are. Alligators and birds both have dinosaur ancestors.

There is a suborder of hollow-boned dinosaurs known as theropods. Modern birds originate from a subgroup of theropods known as the coelurosauria. The coelurosauria were the colloquial strange birds of their day: they were literally feathered dinosaurs. At some point during the Jurassic age (145–201 million years ago) their hollow bones and feathers led to flight.

I was trained in the sciences in both undergrad and graduate school. I believe the scientists; I appreciate their rigor, research, and monomaniacal obsessions. Yet, it's enough for me to look into the eyes of a great egret— the black pupil, the amber yellow iris, the singular, far away stare—or see their scaled, stilted, reptilian legs and know the bird carries something beyond its own history, something beyond history.

Some days I watch them and a world unfolds within me.

*

I've long been fascinated by a spiritual term developed by Gregory of Nyssa in his book *The Life of Moses*. A fourth century theologian and contemplative, Gregory of Nyssa lived in Cappadocia, present-day Turkey. Alongside his brother Basil the Great and their close friend Gregory of Nazianzus, Gregory was one of the Cappadocian Fathers—early Christian theologians influential in the West and East, notably for their work on the Trinity. Macrina the Younger, Gregory and Basil's sister, was a prominent figure in her own right and is now a saint in both the Catholic and Orthodox churches.

The Life of Moses recounts Moses' life from a narrative perspective and then, in the second section, interprets that life as it relates to the mystical, or contemplative, path. Throughout the book Gregory of Nyssa discusses, and wrestles with, the concept of epektasis, a term which claims the spiritual life moves continuously, and eternally, toward God. For Gregory there is no perfect spiritual state to be reached or achieved, but rather the journey, in and of itself, becomes the perfect.

Epektasis envisions our lives as a continuous journey informed by occasional brushes against a reality grander than our own. Each encounter expands our horizons as our sense of reality is transfigured into something deeper, broader, and more mysterious. We are given a few more words, becoming ever more proficient in the language of life.

*

In 19ᵗʰ-century Germany, in the small Bavarian town Eichstätt, a farmer is out in his fields. Something sticking out of the ground catches his eyes and he bends down to pick it up. After some effort he dislodges what is no ordinary piece of limestone but a fossil. And the fossil isn't any ordinary fossil—it looks like the remains of a miniature gryphon or a gremlin with wings. The farmer, Jakob Niemeyer, holds on to the fossil for a year.

Eventually, though, Jakob sells it to his friend the innkeeper Johann Dörr who puts it up in the inn as a novelty item. With the money from the sale Jakob buys a cow. The bizarre fossil hangs on the wall of the inn, uninterpreted. It changes hands a few more times until finally it is purchased in an auction by Museum für Naturkunde, Berlin's Natural History Museum, with help from the industrialist Ernst Werner von Siemens.

The fossil is described as being of the genus *Archaeopteryx*, a combination of the Greek words for "ancient" and "wing." This fossil is the most complete of its kind, not only a full body but an entirely intact head—a first. And the bird, called Urvogel—"first bird"—in German, is a transition species, the species that links feathered yet flightless dinosaurs to our modern birds. Known in full as *Archaeopteryx lithographica*, it was the size of a raven and could fly, though most likely not for long.

I often think of Jakob and if he would have wanted the bird back if told of its historical significance—one of the most important fossil finds to date. Maybe he would have sold it again and bought even more cows. Maybe he would have just said *no, I'm good*. An ordinary farmer in an ordinary town who will be remembered forever because of a stone he found one day.

I think, too, of the bird, the fossil—

Urvogel
Archaeopterex lithographica
First Bird
ἀρχαῖος πτέρυξ

In many ways the bird appears alive, it is not only a complete skeleton but seems to have just jumped off the ground to test its wings, and suddenly realizing it can fly gives off a shriek for something new it has brought to the world. And now, 145 million or so years later, it sits in a museum in Berlin, splayed in stone, frozen in eternity, still crying the scream of transition.

*

I recently moved back to Florida after three years in New Jersey. A few months after returning, in October, I went to a Publix grocery store down the street from my parents' house. When I parked, I discovered a great egret on the hood of the car next to me.

The area between a bird's eyes and its bill is called a lore. When great egrets are breeding their lores turn a bright lime green. This particular great egret was preening itself on the truck's hood, its lore a stripe of neon green like some twenty-year-old headed to a rave.

I walked through the aisles of Publix mindlessly placing vegetables, fruit, and other items into my cart, thinking about that bird. Of all the places it could be it's in a parking lot, surrounded by busy streets and indifferent grocery store patrons, standing on a car hood.

That bird should be in some wetland far, far from here, surrounded by cypress swamps older than Christ.

*

A large part of my youth was spent killing animals. I hesitate to say "hunt" because much of it was simply target practice. It pains me to write these words now; I flinch to recall every BB and bullet pelting the body of bird, rabbit, squirrel. Occasionally, my memory lines these animals up—along with all the deer, hogs, and racoons, too—and I relive each death I caused. My boundaries of concern were so insular and well-kept.

Once, at a friend's ranch, birds flocked by the hundreds to a nearby landfill. The winter sun laid its soft light across the bahiagrass pastures and pine flats as the birds' shadows drifted slowly across it all. We shot the birds from the sky one by one—seagulls, egrets, whatever crossed our path—their lifeless bodies barreling back down to this terrible earth.

With no respect for life, we like little gods took it.

*

Sometimes I see egrets and think of them as lining out evolution like the VHS tapes I forgot to rewind as a child. Some martial arts movie—a broken man's graceful, violent redemption—I'd seen a thousand times. The next kid starts it and sees the end.

*

I imagine God laughing.

The First Bird clumsy as a chick, body slathered in vibrant awkward feathers, runs then jumps only to soar into a hard crash, its bill diving deep into Jurassic earth. But this is Urvogel and it contains the future and sets out again as God's laughter reverberates.

So, again. But this time the jump becomes a glide then a push down with clawed wings, the creature moving upward, the lift streaming stomach, DNA imprinting something that will be so simple for a Great Egret millions of years later.

It must've been sunset. The small raven-like dinosaur-bird's body a silhouette against the reddish-orange dusk, floating momentarily over primeval forest that never knew ax—the giant, deep green leaves.

*

History is dotted with strange figures who exceed the bounds of a singular vocation. One such figure is Lord Northbourne, born in Britain in 1896. Walter Ernest Christopher James, 4th Baron Northbourne studied agriculture at Oxford and rowed on the crew. He eventually rowed in the 1920 summer Olympics, earning a silver medal.

After university Northbourne combined his agricultural science studies with the biodynamic agricultural theory of Rudolph Steiner—another one of history's eccentric polymaths. Northbourne soon became a leading opponent of the burgeoning industrialized agricultural movement that would later become known as the Green Revolution. The agriculture Northbourne and others promoted envisioned the land as a living entity that demanded care and respect. Lord Northbourne is credited with creating the term "organic farming" and his book *Look to the Land*, alongside his advocacy, is considered seminal in the field.

Yet, rowing and farming were not the end of his pursuits. Northbourne later became associated with the Perennial Philosophy, also known as the Traditionalist school—a loose group of thinkers from various traditions who believe all religious and spiritual traditions seek after the same truth. Northbourne went on to become a scholar of comparative religion and wrote widely on the subject.

Northbourne's writings, many collected in *Of the Land & the Spirit*, seek to find a way to combine his deep interests in the material and spiritual. Suspicious of the modern distinction between mind and body, Northbourne questioned the prevailing industrial mentality and drew attention to the growing reductionism of the scientific outlook, which privileged the empirical: "In fact, it is much more how we see things than what we see."

I often stumble in trying to walk a line between respecting the power and validity of science, while not falling prey to its reductive dogmatism. Northbourne's words have always served as a dependable guide. They capture those moments beyond explanation that are, yet, too powerful to dismiss: "Whatever is too exalted or too comprehensive to be grasped or defined distinctively, though it can in principle be apprehended directly."

*

I have sat waist-deep in a swamp pond, surrounded by alligator flag and frogbit, shadowed by cypress limbs draped in Spanish moss. I have heard the great egret's slow shriek, the strange mix of hissed air and the tear of a palmetto blade, the prehistoric lurch of a great blue heron, the warbling roll of sandhill cranes. I have been taken to places I have never been.

*

As Gregory of Nyssa knew well, we never completely reach the absolute, the fullness of being, God—instead we are graced with moments of egrets in mangrove tunnels or baby gators in the hand. Wakeful moments that shake our limits and expand the world as we know it. Like springs in their excessiveness, they overflow with meaning, never yielding boundary or bottom.

Yet, there is a distinction to these moments I have long struggled to express. The egret in the mangroves is a different experience than the egret striking its prey at Corkscrew Swamp. While both experiences are transcendent, the transcendence is of a different type.

I have long categorized these events as ecstatic. The Greek word ἔκστασις (*ekstasis*), root of the English words ecstasy and ecstatic, is the combination of two words—the Greek words for "out" and "I stand." At its root, ecstasy means to stand outside of oneself, perfectly capturing those moments of revelation, of epiphany, wherein we are amazed, dazed, and, as the saying goes, beside ourselves.

Yet, this etymology only seems appropriate for those moments when one transcends the world as time's procession ceases and all else fades away before an overwhelming feeling often called religious or spiritual. But what of the other moments, the moments when one is brought within a reality beneath the superficial monotony of the everyday?

These experiences are transcendent in another way—they awaken us to a depth lurking under the surface of the quotidian. They are not a rising above, or outside of, life but a deepening into it. I've come to call these moments *entostatic*—utilizing the Greek preposition ἐντός (*entos*), meaning within or inside. Entostatic are those transcendent experiences where I don't stand outside myself but, rather, come more profoundly into myself, and this world, through a heightened perception of all things. My connection to my body and the world is felt in its fullness.

Two moments—observing the great egret's stillness before it struck its prey and holding the baby alligator at the farm—awoke me to something beyond the ephemeral happenings of this world, something primitive. And this isn't some nostalgic romanticism; I'm not trying to capture a specific past but rather something primal that pulses in the here and now.

The entostatic moments provide a living connection to a place before words.

*

When I was in elementary school, I'd regularly visit a friend who lived near Tampa Bay. Most days we'd wander down his street to play along a rock-strewn seawall by the ocean's lapping waves. Occasionally, we were joined by a neighborhood kid whose name I've forgotten; I only remember he always had a white shirt on.

One day the three of us headed to the bay's edge. The homes in the area had large yards and the space by the water was relatively private. We picked up rocks and broken glass and threw them into the sea. At some point, the kid with the white shirt pulled bread from his pocket and tossed out small pieces until a parade of seagulls descended upon us. He then stuck his hand back in his pocket and removed a tiny white disk.

I will never forget his face as he grinned, told me it was Alka-Seltzer, and then stuffed it into a larger piece of bread. He threw the piece into the crowd of birds, and it was instantaneously swiped up by a seagull. A deranged smile appeared across his face, *Its belly's going to explode.*

I cringed as it flew away, imagining this white-feathered bomb igniting in the distance.

In my mind that bird still flies fast over ocean. Its never-ending journey becomes a repentance, calling me outward, away from all the death I've created.

*

One Friday afternoon in college my friend Adam and I loaded my canoe—the same blue Mad River—onto my two-door Chevy Blazer and left Gainesville for the Sante Fe River. Our friend Chris had a river house in Sante Fe, twenty minutes or so north of Gainesville, and we were going to meet him for the weekend.

At some point along I-75 our conversation ceased, and I zoned out as one does while driving. It must've been spring then, I remember the trees—the chlorophyll seemed to burst forth from the leaves to create this shimmering green mass. The trees lining both sides of the interstate suddenly overwhelmed me. My skin tingled with energy that covered my entire body like a blanket. I was wrapped up in it and felt charged. Driving down a highway hungover, the trees tilted down to me, trying to talk to me with words beyond my own tongue.

In that entostatic moment—Adam beside me, completely unaware—I shut it out. I closed it off with all my might. Immediately the sensation disappeared.

I'd entered the slipstream for a second, was inundated with all the world had to share, and a second later stopped it. I was paralyzed with wonder and, yet, was terrorized by it.

Maybe I wasn't ready to give myself to that mystery. Maybe I thought I didn't deserve it.

*

Sometimes when I see a great egret, I watch them for a few seconds; perhaps they lift their head and look my way, and then I say, silently, *I could never put you in a cage.*

*

In the Victorian era, in cosmopolitan cities like New York City, Paris, or London, women walked around wearing large hats decorated with plumes. These plumes were not synthetic but rather real feathers from real birds: snowy egrets, spoonbills, flamingos, great egrets. As with many fashion trends, it looked silly *and* ornate, ridiculous *and* prestigious.

The feathers these women wore were acquired through simple acts: birds were shot, their showy feathers removed. The majority of these plumes were taken from birds in the Everglades of South Florida. Estimates indicate plume hunters were killing more than five million birds a year in the Everglades alone. Populations of wading and shore birds dropped to dangerously low numbers.

The demand for fashionable plumes became so outrageous that certain feathers were worth twice their weight in gold. No feather was more desired than the breeding plumage of snowy egrets (*Egretta thula*). When the breeding season arrives, snowy egrets grow long, slender white plumes all over their neck, head, and back. These delicate, wispy feathers were the most prized, and their popularity led to the near extinction of snowy egrets.

During the dry season in South Florida, water becomes a rare commodity. The once expansive waters recede and fish pool up into the small remaining bodies of water. This creates an easy feast and wading birds descend across the greater Everglades to feed, breed, and nest. Plume hunters would gather there too, to shoot, kill, and take. Numerous young birds were left to die of starvation as the bullet-ridden bodies of their parents lay deserted across the earth.

The tide began to slowly turn, though, as many folks realized bird populations couldn't sustain the plume industry's rabid demand. One of the first game wardens in all of America was hired at this time, specifically to protect birds from plume hunters. His name was Guy Bradley.

Bradley moved with his family to Florida from Chicago as a child. Growing up in South Florida, the young Bradley served as a guide for plume hunters, among them the famed French hunter Jean Chevalier. Chevalier was notorious for his hunting exploits. Gloria Jahoda, one of Florida's greatest chroniclers, mentions in her book *River of the Golden Ibis* that during a particular hunt, "One of Chevalier's boatmen saw a kill of a thousand egrets in a single day." By the time he was eighteen, Bradley himself would have killed, or guided others in the killing of, thousands upon thousands of birds. All pillaged for their feathers, their disrobed carcasses left to rot.

Eventually laws were passed to protect the birds and other wildlife, and Bradley left his plume hunting ways behind him. He was hired by the Florida Audubon Society—whose namesake also killed so many birds—to protect plume birds across an expansive range reaching down to the Florida Keys.

What led Guy Bradley, this rough, tough, sun-squinted blue-eyed man, to live in the most uninhabitable of places, all to look after birds?

Most accounts quote Bradley saying the recent legislation outlawing plume hunting was motivation for his new line of work. It had to be more complex than just a change in laws, though. This man had made money hand over fist killing birds. His memory was riddled with image after image of plume-robbed bodies, a never-ending ticker tape of dead birds killed for a few feathers.

Certain times I imagine Guy Bradley doing his solitary work—a miserable and extremely dangerous way to live. Many poachers wouldn't hesitate to kill anyone that tried to stop them; a hard reality Bradley learned three years later. I see him out there tromping through the Glades, protecting these birds but also filling his mind with new memories. He combs the swamps, woods, and marshes seeking image after image of living bird—snowy egrets, spoonbills, flamingos, great egrets. Each day the warden walks no longer toward death, and each bird he sees—neck arched over their young nestlings to feed, flying through the pale South Florida sky, or wading through tannin-stained swamp water—becomes a sort of resurrection.

*

I still see egrets regularly. I see them along roadways eating from drainage ditches, down creeks off the Chassahowitzka River, hopping from the brick of a neighborhood road onto the yard behind them, flying overhead. Their stark white bodies bring pause and the world around them slips away. Other times, the egret's presence transforms all that surrounds it, and a deeper sense is brought to the world.

Great egrets are not so much totem, sign, or symbol; they are each a unique, singular bird carrying within themselves the story of this world. They invite us, occasionally, into that story and we carry forth as the salty red liquid that pumps through the world. We follow a history unbound by the strictures of time and become what has always and will always be.

*

Bird, bark your cry.

Originally published in North American Review

Cooper Young

Behind the Buddha

A narrow path bends
around the main temple
to a modest shrine
beside a grave. Cracks
line the stone walls,
and mosquitos
rest on the eyes
of a golden Buddha.
On the ground, ants
surround the body
of a dragonfly.
They take away
sapphire scales,
leaving nothing
but a shell
and a shadow.

Originally published in Shō Poetry Journal

ACKNOWLEDGMENTS & PERMISSIONS

"ISM" copyright © 2023 by Sarah Ghazal Ali. Reprinted from *Guernica* by permission of the author.

"Pantoum with Ecclesiastes" copyright © 2023 by Sarah Ghazal Ali. Reprinted from *The Sewanee Review* (#CXXXI.2) by permission of the author.

"Like a Prayer" copyright © 2024 by Sionnain Buckley.

"Duns Scotus" copyright © 2023 by James Roderick Burns. Reprinted from *Vita Poetica* (Summer 2023) by permission of the author.

"Overtures on Some Unanswered Questions" copyright © 2023 by Mark Christhilf. Reprinted from *The Potomac Review* (#73) by permission of the author.

"Cathedral" copyright © 2023 by Kwame Dawes. Reprinted from *The Adroit Journal* (#44) by permission of the author.

"Velar" copyright © 2023 by Moira Egan. Reprinted from *The Hopkins Review* (#16.2) by permission of the author.

"A Reverence" copyright © 2023 by Jeff Hardin. Reprinted from *The Ilanot Review* (#26.1) by permission of the author.

"Rumi and the Clock of Shams Tabrizi" copyright © 2023 by Shadab Zeest Hashmi. Reprinted from *3 Quarks Daily* by permission of the author.

"A Story About the Body" copyright © 1990 by Robert Hass. Reprinted from *Human Wishes* by permission of Ecco Press. All rights reserved.

"Litany" copyright © 2024 by Kristin Kovacic.

"On Robert Hass's 'A Story About the Body'" copyright © 2023 by Dana Levin. Reprinted from *Poetry Daily* by permission of the author.

Acknowledgments & Permissions

"Grief-Keeping" copyright © 2023 by Minadora Macheret. Reprinted from *Brevity* (#73) by permission of the author.

"Cinder 136" copyright © 2023 by Ray Malone. Reprinted from *Star 82 Review* (#11.2) by permission of the author.

"The Teachings of Naranja" copyright © 2023 by Mary B. Moore. Reprinted from *Birmingham Poetry Review* (#50) by permission of the author.

"Bone Lab" copyright © 2023 by Marilyn Moriarty. Reprinted from *Dappled Things* (#18.4) by permission of the author.

"A Homily" & "Night Drive" copyright © 2023 by Kylan Rice. Reprinted from *Brink Literary Journal* (Spring 2023) by permission of the author.

"The Shammes" copyright © 2023 by Matthue Roth. Reprinted from *The Cincinatti Review* (#20.1) by permission of the author.

"Mary Magdalene on Sunday" copyright © 2024 by Merryn Rutledge.

"Even Now, After all These Years" copyright © 2023 by Heidi Seaborn. Reprinted from *The Missouri Review* (#46.1) by permission of the author.

"A Plague of Locusts" copyright © 2023 by Julie Marie Wade. Reprinted from *Ecotone* (#34) by permission of the author.

"To a Great Egret" copyright © 2023 by Will Wellman. Reprinted from *North American Review* (#308.2) by permission of the author.

"Behind the Buddha" copyright © 2023 by Cooper Young. Reprinted from *Shō Poetry Journal* (#3) by permission of the author.

CONTRIBUTORS

Sarah Ghazal Ali is the author of *Theophanies* (Alice James Books, 2024), selected as the Editors' Choice for The 2022 Alice James Award. A Stadler Fellow and recipient of *The Sewanee Review* poetry prize, her work has appeared in *The American Poetry Review*, *The Kenyon Review*, the Academy of American Poets' *Poem-A-Day* series, and elsewhere. She is the poetry editor for *West Branch* and lives in the Bay Area, California.

Sionnain Buckley is a writer and visual artist based in Columbus. Her work has appeared in *DIAGRAM*, *Wigleaf*, *Strange Horizons*, *Foglifter*, *Autostraddle*, and other places. She holds an MFA in fiction from Ohio State and has received fellowships from The Adirondack Center for Writing, The Seventh Wave, and The Kimmel Harding Nelson Center for the Arts.

James Roderick Burns is the author of one flash fiction collection, *To Say Nothing of the Dog*, and five poetry collections, most recently *Crows at Dusk*; a collection of four novellas, *The Unregulated Heart*, was published in 2024. His stories have twice been nominated for the Pushcart Prize, and he serves as Staff Reader in Poetry for *Ploughshares*. His newsletter "A Bunch of Fives" offers one free, published story a fortnight (abunchoffives.substack.com).

An emeritus professor at Eastern Illinois University, **Mark Christhilf** has published a book of poetry, *Gracious Is the Earth*, and a book of criticism, *W. S. Merwin the Mythmaker*. His poems, essays, and reviews have appeared in numerous journals, including *The Yale Literary Magazine*, *The Atlanta Review*, and *The Midwest Quarterly*. "Overtures on Some Unanswerable Questions" is taken from his yet unpublished book by that title, which also contains his essay "The Essence of Consciousness," recently published in *The Journal of Consciousness Exploration and Research* (13.3). He is currently writing a book on consciousness, "The Creative Yoke."

Kwame Dawes is the author of twenty-five books of poetry and other books of fiction, criticism, and essays. His most recent collection *Sturge Town* (Peepal Tree Press, UK) is a 2023 PBS Autumn Choice. *Sturge Town* appeared in the USA with Norton in 2024. Dawes is a George W. Holmes University Professor of English and Glenna Luschei Editor of *Prairie Schooner*. He teaches in the Pacific MFA Program and is the Series Editor of The African Poetry Book Series, Director of The African Poetry Book Fund, and Artistic Director of The Calabash International Literary Festival. Kwame Dawes is a Fellow of The Royal Society of Literature, the winner of The Windham/Campbell Award for Poetry, and was a finalist for The 2022 Neustadt International Prize for Literature. In 2024, Dawes was named the Poet Laureate of Jamaica.

Moira Egan won The 2023 Raiziss/de Palchi Fellowship from The Academy of American Poets for her translations of Giorgiomaria Cornelio's poetry. Her most recent poetry collection is *Amore e morte*, a bilingual new and selected (Edizioni Tlon, Rome). Her poems and essays have appeared in journals and anthologies on four continents. She lives in Rome with her husband and co-translator, Damiano Abeni.

Jeff Hardin is the author of seven books of poetry, most recently *Watermark*, *A Clearing Space in the Middle of Being*, and *No Other Kind of World*. Recent and forthcoming poems appear in *The Southern Review*, *Image*, *Bennington Review*, *The Laurel Review*, *Zone 3*, *Louisville Review*, *Grist*, and elsewhere. He lives and teaches in TN.

Shadab Zeest Hashmi, a poet and essayist, is the winner of the San Diego Book Award, Sable's Hybrid Book Prize, and the Nazim Hikmet Poetry Prize. Her books include *Baker of Tarifa, Kohl and Chalk, Ghazal Cosmopolitan* and the lyric memoir *Comb*. Zeest Hashmi's poems have been translated into Spanish, Bosnian, Urdu and Turkish, and her work has appeared in *Prairie Schooner, Mudlark, The Cortland Review, POEM, World Literature Today, Verse Daily, Thrush, Wasafiri,* McSweeney's *In the Shape of a Human Body I am Visiting the Earth* and *The Best Asian Poetry 2021* among other publications worldwide.

Merryn Rutledge's poems have appeared widely throughout the world. A collection, *Sweet Juice and Ruby-Bitter Seed*, is available from Kelsay Books. Merryn's sonnet for Julian of Norwich appears in the 2023 commemorative anthology *All Shall Be Well* (Amethyst Press). Merryn teaches poetry craft, reviews poetry books by women (Tupelo Quarterly, Pedestal, Cider Press Review), sings, dances, and works for social justice causes. Writing poems is a third calling, after teaching literature, film studies, and creative writing at Phillips Exeter Academy, and then, with a doctorate in leadership, running a US-based leadership development consulting firm. During that career phase, Merryn›s field research on leadership was published as books, chapters, and in peer-reviewed journals. Merryn lives near Boston, MA.

Kristin Kovacic has received a Pushcart Prize and other awards for her essays, which have been published in magazines such as *Table, Brain Child, Full Grown People*, and others, and collected in the book *History of My Breath*. She is also the author of the poetry chapbook *House of Women* and editor of the anthology *Birth: A Literary Companion*. She lives in the former St. Matthew Slovak Catholic Church on the South Side of Pittsburgh.

Contributors

Dana Levin is the author of five books poetry, most recently *Now Do You Know Where You Are* (Copper Canyon Press), a 2022 *New York Times* Notable Book and NPR "Book We Love." Recent poems and essays have appeared in *Poem-a-Day*, *Best American Poetry*, *The American Poetry Review*, and *Poetry*, among other publications. She is a grateful recipient of many honors, including those from The National Endowment for the Arts, PEN, and The Library of Congress, as well as from the Rona Jaffe, Whiting, and Guggenheim Foundations. With Adele Elise Williams, she co-edited *Bert Meyers: On the Life and Work of an American Master* (2023) for the Unsung Masters Series. Levin serves as Distinguished Writer in Residence at Maryville University in St. Louis.

Minadora Macheret is a Herbert Post-Doctoral Fellow at the University of Tennessee, Knoxville. She received her PhD from the University of North Texas. A recipient of The James Merrill Poetry Fellowship from Vermont Studio Center, Macheret's work has appeared in *Brevity*, *Salamander*, *Tinderbox Poetry Journal*, and elsewhere. She is the author of the poetry chapbook *Love Me, Anyway* (Porkbelly Press, 2018).

Ray Malone is an Irish writer and artist living in Berlin, Germany, working on a series of projects exploring the lyric potential of minimal forms based on various musical and/or literary models. His work has been published in numerous journals in the US, UK, and Ireland.

Mary B. Moore's forthcoming poetry collection *Amanda Chimera*, winner of The Arthur Smith Award, will be out in 2025 from Madville Publishing. Her latest poetry book is *Dear If* (Orison Books, 2022); earlier books include *Flicker*, *The Book Of Snow*, and the prize-winning chapbooks *Amanda and the Man Soul* and *Eating the Light*. Her poems have appeared or are forthcoming in *Poetry*, *Artemis*, *Catamaran*, *Birmingham Poetry*

Review, NELLE, Nimrod, and more. Moore received *Birmingham Poetry Review*'s 2023 Collins Prize, *NELLE*'s 2019 Three Sisters Award, and the Second Place award in *Nimrod*'s 2017 Pablo Neruda Prize.

Marilyn Moriarty is the author of a textbook on scientific writing, *Writing Science through Critical Thinking,* and a nonfiction book, *Moses Unchained,* which won The Associated Writing Programs' creative nonfiction award. Her essays have been published in *The Antioch Review, The Chattahoochee Review, Creative Nonfiction, Dappled Things, The Kenyon Review, Raritan, River Teeth,* and other journals. She has won several writing contests, among them The 2014 Faulkner-Wisdom Gold Medal for the essay. Three essays have been named "Notable" from the editors of *The Best American Essays* series. She is a professor of English and Creative Writing at Hollins University in Roanoke, Virginia. Her memoir will be published by North Georgia University Press in 2026.

Kylan Rice is the author of the poetry collection *An Image Not a Book* (Free Verse Editions, 2023) and the essay collection *Incryptions* (Spuyten Duyvil, 2021). With Dan Beachy-Quick, he is co-author of *Primer* (Free Poetry, 2023), a collection of conversations about poetics, and he co-edited *Southern Lights: 75 Years of the Carolina Quarterly* (UNC Press, 2023). His creative writing has appeared in *Colorado Review, Denver Quarterly, Image, Kenyon Review Online, Seneca Review, West Branch,* and other journals. He is the associate editor of *The Missouri Review* and co-editor of Thirdhand Books.

Matthue Roth is the author of *Never Mind the Goldbergs,* a Hasidic punk road trip novel which was a NYPL, ALA, and YALSA Best Books nominee, and the picture book *My First Kafka.* "The Shammes" is the first chapter of a new novel. Roth lives with his family in Brooklyn.

Contributors

Merryn Rutledge's poems have appeared widely throughout the world. A collection, *Sweet Juice and Ruby-Bitter Seed*, is available from Kelsay Books. She teaches poetry craft, reviews poetry books by women, sings, dances, and works for social justice causes. Writing poems is a third calling, after teaching literature, film studies, and creative writing at Phillips Exeter Academy, and then, with a doctorate in leadership, running a US-based leadership development consulting firm. During that career phase, Rutledge's field research on leadership was published as books, chapters, and in peer-reviewed journals.

Heidi Seaborn is Executive Editor of *The Adroit Journal* and is the author of three award-winning books/chapbooks of poetry: *An Insomniac's Slumber Party with Marilyn Monroe*, *Give a Girl Chaos*, and *Bite Marks*. A recipient of The *Missouri Review* Jeffrey E. Smith Editors' Prize in Poetry, her work has recently appeared in *Agni*, *Blackbird*, *Copper Nickel*, *diode*, *The Financial Times of London*, *Penn Review*, *Pleiades*, *Poetry Northwest*, *Plume*, *Rattle*, *The Slowdown*, and elsewhere.

Julie Marie Wade is the author of many collections of poetry, prose, and hybrid forms, most recently *Fugue: An Aural History* (Diagram/New Michigan Press, 2023) and *Otherwise: Essays* (Autumn House, 2023), selected by Lia Purpura as the winner of The 2022 Autumn House Nonfiction Book Prize. A winner of The Marie Alexander Poetry Series and The Lambda Literary Award for Lesbian Memoir, Wade teaches in the creative writing program at Florida International University and makes her home with Angie Griffin and their two cats in Dania Beach. Her newest project is *The Mary Years*, winner of The 2023 Clay Reynolds Novella Prize, selected by Michael Martone and released by Texas Review Press in 2024.

Will Wellman is a writer and poet living in Nashville, Tennessee. His nonfiction has been published in *North American Review*, *Bitter Southerner*, and *America*, and was chosen as a "Best of 2020: Science & Nature" by *Longreads*. His poetry has been published in *Plume*, *Journal of American Medical Association*, *The Florida Review*, and elsewhere. He is at work on his first novel.

Cooper Young is a cyber security consultant, poet, and mathematician who hails from Santa Cruz, California. His most recent work has appeared in *California Quarterly*, *Urthona*, *Hawai'i Pacific Review*, and *Shō Poetry Journal*. His chapbook, *Sacred Grounds*, was published by Finishing Line Press in May 2020.

ABOUT THE EDITORS

Luke Hankins is the founder and editor of Orison Books. He is the author of two full-length poetry collections, *Radiant Obstacles* and *Weak Devotions*, as well as a chapbook, *Testament* (Texas Review Press, 2023). He is also the author of a collection of essays, *The Work of Creation*, and is the editor or co-editor of several anthologies, including *Poems of Devotion: An Anthology of Recent Poets* and *Between Paradise & Earth: Eve Poems* (with Nomi Stone). A volume of his translations from the French of Stella Vinitchi Radulescu, *A Cry in the Snow & Other Poems*, was published by Seagull Books in 2018.

Nathan Poole is the author of two books of fiction, *Father Brother Keeper* (Sarabande Books, 2015), a collection of stories selected by Edith Pearlman for the 2013 Mary McCarthy Prize and long-listed for the Frank O'Connor Award, and *Pathkiller as the Holy Ghost*, selected by Benjamin Percy as the winner of the 2014 *Quarterly West* Novella Contest. He has been awarded The *Narrative* Prize, a Milton Fellowship at *Image*, and a Joan Beebe Fellowship at Warren Wilson College.

Karen Tucker is the author of the novel *Bewilderness* (Catapult, 2021), which was selected as a "Dazzling Debut" by the American Booksellers Association and was longlisted for the Aspen Words Literary Prize. Tucker's short fiction can be found in *The Missouri Review*, *The Yale Review*, *Boulevard*, *EPOCH*, *Tin House*, and elsewhere. The recipient of an Elizabeth George Foundation Grant for Emerging Writers and a PEO Scholar Award, she teaches fiction and creative nonfiction at UNC Chapel Hill.

ABOUT ORISON BOOKS

Orison Books is a 501(c)3 non-profit literary press focused on the life of the spirit from a broad and inclusive range of perspectives. We seek to publish books of exceptional poetry, fiction, and non-fiction from perspectives spanning the spectrum of spiritual and religious thought, ethnicity, gender identity, and sexual orientation.

As a non-profit literary press, Orison Books depends on the support of donors. To find out more about our mission and our books, or to make a donation, please visit www.orisonbooks.com.

Orison Books is deeply grateful to our recurring annual donors for sustaining our important work. If you'd like to make a recurring or one-time contribution, please visit www.orisonbooks.com/support-us.

Sustainers' Circle

Carol Dines
Michele Laub
Laura & Barry Rand
Bruce Spang
Anonymous

Advocates' Circle

David Ebenbach
Anonymous

Supporters' Circle

Nickole Brown
Richard Chess

Friends' Circle

Paige Gilchrist
Laurel Haavik
Alida Woods